# SWIM
# SPEED
## *STROKES*

### FOR SWIMMERS AND TRIATHLETES

# SWIM SPEED

# STROKES

## FOR SWIMMERS AND TRIATHLETES

MASTER BUTTERFLY, BACKSTROKE,
BREASTSTROKE, AND FREESTYLE FOR YOUR
FASTEST SWIMMING

# SHEILA TAORMINA

Boulder, Colorado

**▼velopress®**

3002 Sterling Circle, Suite 100
Boulder, Colorado 80301-2338 USA
(303) 440-0601 · Fax (303) 444-6788 · E-mail velopress@competitorgroup.com

Distributed in the United States and Canada by Ingram Publisher Services

A Cataloging-in-Publication record for this book is available from the Library of Congress.
ISBN: 978-1-937715-21-2

For information on purchasing VeloPress books,
please call (800) 811-4210, ext. 2138, or visit www.velopress.com.

This paper meets the requirements of ANSI/NISO Z39.48-1992 (Permanence of Paper).

Cover design by Lora Lamm
Interior design and composition by Anita Koury
Photography by Daniel Smith
Photo editing by Nick Salazar and Paula Gillen
Photographs on p. 82 (Fig. 4.8) and p. 127 (Fig. 7.1) courtesy of
Indiana University, Counsilman Center for the Science of Swimming
Illustration on p. 69 by Nicole Kaufman

Text set in Chronicle

14   15   16 / 10   9   8   7   6   5   4   3   2   1

To Vincent de Maio, Kathleen Jeffs,
and swimmers on the Clovis Swim Team in Clovis, New Mexico.
It has been a pleasure to watch you practice deliberately and purposefully.

(Drinking triple-shot lattes with you is a pleasure too.)

# CONTENTS

# FOREWORD

I will never forget watching Sheila swim for the first time at the 1996 Olympic Trials. I was doing the TV commentary with my partner Dan Hicks, and we couldn't get over how all the other swimmers towered over Sheila. I recall worrying that she might get washed away by the huge waves that everyone would soon create in the pool, especially off the turns. But to my surprise and many others', she proved me utterly wrong and made her first Olympic team in that final of the 200 freestyle. The number-one reason? She had one of the most beautiful strokes from a technical standpoint that I had ever seen on a swimmer. She went on to win a gold medal at those Atlanta Games, and I was so proud of her not only for her incredible tenacity in the water but also for her great leadership out of the pool. At 5'2", Sheila is an incredible inspiration, and when I speak to groups of kids, which I do every year, I use Sheila as a shining example that you don't have to be a giant to succeed in this sport.

Sheila has taken all the knowledge she has gained and refined throughout a phenomenal career and brought it to the book you now hold in your hands, *Swim Speed Strokes*. It is a swim training bible that concentrates on teaching technique in all four competitive strokes, featuring fantastic over- and under-water crystal-clear photos of world-class elites. However, the lessons here are not taught in a dry, encyclopedic way. Far from it. Rather, my friend Sheila brings her energetic, encouraging, whip-smart personality to her coaching, which is why this book is so enjoyable and educational. She's truly a one-of-a-kind coach!

Undoubtedly, talent helps with success in swimming, but it is precision, practice, and dedication that are most important. This book is filled with examples from world-class athletes who exemplify this. But none more than Sheila. During my own photo shoot for this book, I was deeply impressed by how much attention to detail Sheila gave to every single shot. She is precision and dedication in action.

I've never met a person with so much enthusiasm for the sport of swimming. That love shines through on every page of this book. I am honored to be included, and I know readers will be thrilled with the results they see in their own swimming after having read it.

Swim fast!

*—Rowdy Gaines*

# ACKNOWLEDGMENTS

There exists a strong culture of solidarity in the sport of swimming. Coaches and athletes openly share knowledge and give their time generously. Without such spirit, this book would have never lifted from the ground. The first nod of gratitude therefore goes to those who came onboard with this project, and who did so enthusiastically. You are champions on and off the pool deck.

To the athletes: Elizabeth Beisel, Nicolas Fink, Rowdy Gaines, Andrew Gemmell, Ariana Kukors, Melanie Margalis, Vladimir Morozov, Aaron Peirsol, Doug Reynolds, Laura Sogar, Rebecca Soni, Peter Vanderkaay, and Ashley Whitney.

To the coaches: Dave Salo, Jon Urbanchek, and Catherine Vogt of the University of Southern California; Jack Bauerle and Harvey Humphries of the University of Georgia; Gregg Troy and Martyn Wilby of the University of Florida; and Carol Capitani of the University of Texas.

To the athletes and coaches interviewed for their valuable insights on technique: Maritza Correia, Annette Salmeen, Nelson Diebel, Kathy Coffin-Sheard, Matt Kredich of the University of Tennessee, Ray Looze of Indiana University, and Russell Mark of USA Swimming.

To those who offered their time, resources, and facilities in support of this project: Ross Bohlken, general manager at Heathrow Country Club in Lake Mary, Florida; Bob and Ian Thomsen at the Georgia Aquatic Center in Watkinsville, Georgia; Lizet Fiol at the Palmas de Cortez in Los Barriles, Mexico;

Tom Rau and Craig Askins of Hamburg, Michigan; Eva Solomon of Ann Arbor, Michigan; Steve Flippen of the University of Georgia Athletic Department; Daniel Seigel of the University of Florida Athletic Department; Marissa Kleber, sports agent; Pirie Humphries of Athens, Georgia; John Bathurst and Jack Coffey at Speedo; Lisa Jayne of Reno, Nevada; and Jeff and Jill Cole of San Diego, California.

To Bruce Wigo, executive director of the International Swimming Hall of Fame, and your wonderful staff—Marion Washburn, Marcia Meiners, Ivonne Schmid, Laurie Marchwinski, and Bob Duenkel—for preserving swimming history and welcoming me for six weeks to your amazing library to research and write.

To Mike Unger of USA Swimming for helping me launch this project at the 2013 USA Swimming National Championships in Indianapolis.

To Dave Tanner of Indiana University for sharing your expertise and providing Doc's photographic media of Rowdy Gaines, and to Jay Kinca for helping prepare the media for print.

To John Erdman of Clovis, New Mexico, for preparing video images for print.

To two very special coaches I had at a young age: Ms. Patricia Poirier, who could cite Bernoulli's Principle early in her career as a teenage coach, and Mr. Gordon Larson, whose Wednesday night drill sessions were purposefully designed to develop proper mechanics in his swimmers' strokes. I am fortunate to have trained under your watchful eyes early in my swimming career.

To Daniel Smith, photographer on this project, for once again spending hours underwater to capture the most beautiful images—and for making it fun every minute.

To Ernie Maglischo, whose work I admire more than any in the field. Warm thanks also to Jan Rendtorff for her hospitality while Ernie and I talked swimming for hours.

Finally, to the staff at VeloPress—Ted Costantino, Casey Blaine, Renee Jardine, Haley Berry, Dave Trendler, Vicki Hopewell, and Anita Koury—it is an honor to team with you on a third book. My admiration and thankfulness grows deeper with every project. Special thanks to Haley Berry for your adventurous spirit on the drive down the Baja, and to Casey Blaine, my editor, for overseeing each step of the way with confidence and a clear vision—I couldn't imagine writing a word without your input. Great synergy cannot be crafted; it just has to be.

# INTRODUCTION

**HAVE YOU HEARD** of the 10,000-hour rule? It's the rule that says the key to mastering a complex task is to practice it for 10,000 hours. The quick math on this is if you practice 50 weeks of the year, for 20 hours per week, then you will have logged 10,000 hours at the 10-year point. At that point you should—or could -be an expert at whatever you are practicing. The concept was popularized by Malcolm Gladwell in his best-selling book *Outliers*.

In *Outliers* Gladwell cites numerous examples of the rule. He points to the fact that the Beatles performed in Germany more than 1,200 times over the span of five years in the early 1960s, helping to boost their total playing time to over 10,000 hours before they became a worldwide sensation. And Microsoft founder Bill Gates had access to a computer lab at the local high school and spent countless hours as a teenager—at least 10,000—programming on it. Gladwell cites grand master chess players and elite violinists who have also put in the time.

K. Anders Ericsson, the Florida State University psychologist whose research on the topic of expertise is the basis for Gladwell's book, explains that skill acquisition is not just about logging the hours, however. Those who master a complex skill—whether it be swinging a golf club, playing the piano, or becoming a surgeon, teacher, or accountant—achieve their mastery through what Ericsson terms *deliberate practice*. They engage in highly structured activities and practice tasks that are specifically intended to improve performance. In other words, expert performers don't just show up to practice and go through the motions; they understand their domain and train with great purpose.

Competitive swimming is definitely a complex task. The arms pull back and recover forward; the legs kick; the core moves in momentum with the stroke; and in the midst of it all, the swimmer negotiates clearing the head from the

## MY 10,000 HOURS

When I read Gladwell's book, I was curious to calculate how many cumulative hours I spent swimming before making my first Olympic team, and I was surprised to find that I fit snugly into the 10,000-hour rule. I based my calculations on practicing 50 weeks of the year and came up with the following:

| AGE RANGE | HOURS/WEEK | HOURS/YEAR | AGE-RANGE TOTAL |
|---|---|---|---|
| 6–10 | 4 | 200 | 1,000 |
| 11–15 | 10 | 500 | 2,500 |
| 16–25 | 15 | 750 | 7,500 |
| 26–27.5 | 20 | 1,000 | 1,500 |
| | | | TOTAL: 12,500 |

**Age 16:** first junior national cut-off time (after ~4,000 hours of training)
**Age 17:** first senior national cut-off time (~5,000 hours)
**Age 18:** finals, Division 1 NCAA Championships (~5,750 hours)
**Age 21:** U.S. national team selection, for the World University Games (~8,000 hours)
**Age 27:** 1996 Olympic team (~12,000 hours)

I enjoyed every hour of it (well, *almost* every hour).

water to take a breath. If the thought of swimming for 10,000 hours to master this complex sport has your head spinning, take comfort in the fact that the 10,000-hour rule is a generalization (there are many examples of those who reach expert level in less than 10,000 hours), and it's not 10,000 hours or nothing. High levels of competency are reached in 3,500–6,000 hours, and we can even become quite good at complex tasks in 1,000–2,000 hours, or less.

The key, and the main qualifier in Ericsson's research, is that the practice be deliberate and purposeful.

What is deliberate practice in swimming? It first and foremost involves developing proper technique and mechanics. Swimmers are at the mercy of the laws of physics and fluid dynamics as they stream down the pool. The fastest swimmers in the world move in particular ways, and for good reason--the laws of nature demand it. Strength, speed, and endurance work for swimmers only if there is first a foundation of proper technique.

Technique is where most of the mystery resides in swimming. The better part of the sport takes place in what I call "the deep blue"—beneath the swimmer's body. It is nearly impossible to see what is happening in the deep blue if observing from the pool deck or the spectator seating. And even if a swimmer goes underwater and observes another swimmer from below, the dynamics of the stroke are too much to process all at once. It must be slowed down and digested in pieces if it is to be even partly understood.

I am grateful to James "Doc" Counsilman, who pioneered the art of photographing the underwater elements of the swim stroke more than 60 years ago. His black-and-white pictures showed the strokes of Olympic champions freeze-framed at various phases and unlocked much of the mystery for me. It had a profound impact on my understanding of what to do in the water.

I want to do the same for swimmers today. I want them to see what the best swimmers in the world do underwater. With visuals of top-of-the-line technique seared in the mind, aspiring athletes can train deliberately to adopt the critical mechanics that are present in elite strokes.

I felt strongly, from day one of this project, that the athletes demonstrating the technique for readers should be the Beatles and Bill Gates of the sport: *Each chapter features at least one world-record holder and/or Olympic medalist and is reinforced with photos of national team members and NCAA standouts.* Why is it so important that the best swimmers in the world showcase the strokes? Other than for the obvious reason of being thoroughly inspired by superb human movement, there are many technical reasons why:

- The best swimmers in the world make very few mechanical mistakes. Swimming is a three-dimensional sport with depth components in addition to lateral and fore-aft components, and because of this there is much room for error. While the best in the world are not exempt from making mistakes, they operate on all three dimensions nearly perfectly. So, from a mechanical perspective, you are seeing the best that real-life has to offer.

- The best swimmers in the world are masters at feeling the water. Feeling or "holding" the water in order to gain traction and move the body forward is critical to swimming success, yet can be a difficult concept to grasp and apply. Coaches are even divided as to whether or not a feel for the water can be taught. I wholeheartedly believe it can be and know the impact that great photos can have on turning this concept from abstract to understandable. I took care to ensure the swim strokes in this book were photographed from a variety of unique angles to give readers a glimpse into this mysterious world.

- The best swimmers in the world are simultaneously propulsive and efficient. Every effort that moves an elite swimmer forward in the water is intertwined with a mental feedback loop that signals him or her to feel the flow of water around the body and minimize the resistance caused by that flow. In the photos you will see the art of this dual focus of maximizing propulsion while minimizing drag captured at specific moments in the stroke.

- Finally, the best swimmers in the world are athletes in the water. The two standards by which I measure a swimmer's athleticism are tone and timing.

○ ***Tone.*** Elite swimmers stroke and kick with an ideal level of muscle tension in their arms, legs, and core. They are neither too rigid nor too relaxed. The photos showing this strong tone are my personal favorites.

○ ***Timing.*** I like to sing the praise of Aristotle here, who is credited with the phrase "The whole is greater than the sum of the parts." Each *part* of the swim stroke—the pull, the kick, and the core movement— is a unique and powerful movement in and of itself, but it is the way in which these motions intertwine with one another and emerge as a *whole* that adds a power-packed punch to the swim stroke. The top swimmers in the world understand the connection and timing, and their athleticism in this regard should be noted, studied, and applied.

The photos are unquestionably the main feature of this book. They are almost strong enough to stand on their own—no words needed. But there are two other features in the book that I believe can impart a deliberate and dedicated training mentality for readers: swim science and stroke data.

The book kicks off, in Chapter 1, with a review of swim science. I realize most readers don't pick up a book on swimming because they want to brush up on science. The topic is complicated, lengthy, and admittedly boring. But as I have dug through it in the past few years, I have realized just how closely linked physics—mainly the concepts of fluid dynamics—is with the teachings of stroke mechanics, and I decided that if there was anything that could be done to bring forth the basic principles in a manner that was not intimidating, then it should be done. In this book I have made great effort to condense the science of swimming and present it in a way that I hope is easy for readers to understand. I believe that when swimmers understand the physics, they can capitalize on that understanding to craft a better stroke.

This book also places strong emphasis on a valuable analysis tool called stroke data. Stroke data reveals how well a swimmer translates mechanics and technique into speed and performance. Rather than simply clocking the time it takes to complete a swim, stroke data captures the details underlying the swim, such as the number of strokes an athlete takes to cover a particular distance, and how quickly the athlete takes those strokes. The data is a perfect complement to a swimmer's study of technique, because it is an objective measure of the effectiveness of technique.

While conducting interviews with elite swimmers for this book, I found that more than 90 percent of them could articulate an understanding of stroke data and how it relates to their performance. This high percentage indicated to me that a firm grasp of the tool is closely linked with results at the highest levels. Chapter 4 explains how to gather and use stroke data, and the chapters on butterfly, backstroke, breaststroke, and freestyle include charts that detail the stroke data underlying elite performances in that particular stroke.

There is another thread that runs throughout these pages, and it snuck up on me as I worked on the book: the propulsive similarities among the four strokes.

My first book, *Swim Speed Secrets*, focused solely on the freestyle stroke and the vital elements of the underwater pull—the few things swimmers cannot forgo if they want to get faster. I knew that the vital elements in freestyle are also vital and present in all strokes, but even I was shocked at the extent to which this is the case. My intent with this book was to photograph the underwater mechanics in each stroke, including the most critical elements of it, so swimmers could learn from the sport's icons in their stroke specialty. As each photo session ended, however, and the images downloaded, I saw a striking resemblance among the strokes. I zoomed in on images—focusing on just one arm during a particular phase of the stroke—and noted that the strokes are not only similar, but they are indistinguishable from one another.

To show what I mean, here is a fun test: Each of the four strokes—butterfly, backstroke, breaststroke, and freestyle—is represented in the photos on page 7. Each photo captures the stroke during the catch phase of the pull. The arms you see in these photos are the arms of world-record holders swimming the stroke naturally. None of the photos were staged. Can you match the photo with the stroke?

How did you do? Not an easy test, right? If I wasn't the one to select the photos I'm not sure how I would do. It's a bugger. Don't worry about how you

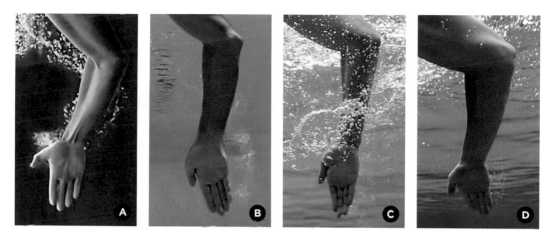

**NAME THAT STROKE.** Identify the stroke for each of the catch phases of the pull shown here.

scored. The key is that you understand through this example how working on the mechanics of any one stroke reinforces the other strokes. I hope this inspires you at practice.

Many swimmers think of themselves as one-stroke, or maybe two-stroke, specialists. The majority of triathletes stick to freestyle, and competitive swimmers slip to the back of the lane at practice when the coach gives a set that involves their weaker strokes. We fall into the trap of thinking, *I'm just not naturally good at that stroke, so why try?*

The stealth message in this book is that putting forth effort in your nonprimary strokes will do you more good than you can imagine. Consider this quote from a triathlete who took a backstroke clinic I coached in the winter of 2014:

> *What stunned me is that learning the correct catch and grab for the backstroke translated into my FINALLY figuring out the catch and grab for freestyle. Who knew that after all these years, it would take flipping me onto my back to get the most important part of the freestyle stroke?*

---

*Note: The photo for backstroke was rotated but otherwise not altered.*

ANSWERS: A: BACKSTROKE. B: FREESTYLE. C: BREASTSTROKE. D: BUTTERFLY

This triathlete now deliberately practices backstroke rather than using it as a stroke to take a rest.

So, let's get going. Let's look at what the best swimmers in the world do underwater. There is quite a bit to study and learn. As you digest the information and take it to the pool, keep in mind that 30 minutes of *deliberate* practice is more beneficial than 3 hours of thrashing.

# 1

## UNDERSTANDING
## THE WHY

**THE SPORT OF SWIMMING** has benefited greatly from the work of a handful of pioneers who have devoted much of their careers to researching the scientific principles that explain how a human body suspended in a liquid medium—water—effectively moves forward and through that medium. Because of their work, nearly every movement we see in the photos in this book makes sense. Even if their work has not yet solidified all the answers, they have gifted the swimming community with a much better understanding of the *why* of swim technique. Why do swimmers move in such particular ways? Is it necessary to do so in order to be effective? Why?

I am a firm believer that when an athlete understands the why behind an action, they become a better athlete. Training sessions are meaningful instead of mundane. A coach's instruction is relevant rather than arbitrary. And photos that were dense with visual cues on first inspection unveil layers of swim science and artistry not noticed before. Everything is more perceptible, immersing the athlete in new and deeper levels of understanding.

So, while there remain questions and debate as to how a swimmer most effectively moves forward, it is worthwhile to take some time to review what has been discovered and learned to date. In this chapter I aim to remove the complexities of the science by focusing on only the parts that inspire a better understanding of the sport and that are directly applicable to a swimmer's daily trek. In my previous book, *Swim Speed Secrets*, I briefly reviewed most of these concepts, but in this book they are examined more thoroughly (stopping before the paralysis by analysis stage though, I promise). The photographs in the upcoming chapters show technique from dimensional angles never published before. When the science and the photos are coupled, swimmers will gain a far better understanding of exactly what is involved in mastering this complex sport.

## THE SCIENCE

Since swimming takes place in water, it makes sense to first give consideration to what water is and how it behaves so we can work around it (and in it) more effectively.

Water is obviously a fluid, but what may not be so obvious is while fluids are not solids, they do have volume and mass and therefore qualify as material. Water therefore is material.

First, consider this statement about **volume**: No two material things can occupy the same space at the same time; this is what it means to have volume. If you step into a tub that is filled to the brim, the water will displace and flow over the sides as you lower into it. You and the water cannot both occupy the same space at the same time. The water yields as you barge in. As one physics web site states, "Fluids are polite; they yield their space relatively easy to other material things, at least when compared to solids. A fluid will get out of your way if you ask it" (physics.org).

Now, consider this statement about **mass**: Material things resist changes to their velocity; this is what it means to have mass. Imagine trying to move a large piece of furniture. The furniture has zero velocity occupying its space on the floor, and according to the definition of mass, it wants to stay that way. If you try to move it (change its velocity), it will feel heavy and difficult to push. It resists you because of its mass. Water, having mass, will do the same thing; it will resist if something tries to move it.

So, we can look at water as a material that has traits—traits that are predictable. We know that water will move, and we also know that it will put up resistance in doing so. Knowing this helps us interact with it more effectively. If we take the study a bit further and learn what the movement and the resistance look like, then we will better understand how to work *with* water to suit our competitive swimming needs.

This is what the men and women who study swim propulsion do. They study how fluids move and resist. Their work is based on established academic principles from the branch of physics known as *fluid dynamics.* Fluid dynamics is the study of fluids in motion, and in particular how fluids flow past an object. A swimmer is an object past which fluids flow, so fluid dynamics is the field that pertains directly to our sport.

Readers who brush up on swim science literature will come across terminology and references familiar from the field of aerodynamics—the study of how *air* flows past objects (airplane flight being the most common). Don't let this confuse you; air is also a fluid, and aerodynamics is a subfield of fluid dynamics.* Many theories carry over from aerodynamics to fluid dynamics, and vice versa, including those pertaining to swim science. It is fortunate for swimmers that this is so, because the image of an airplane flying is recognizable to all, keeping some of the concepts of swim propulsion from becoming too abstract.

In order to take the next step toward understanding swim science and ultimately becoming a better swimmer, let's briefly visit the field of fluid dynamics. This base knowledge will take us to the theories of propulsion that have

---

* The scope of fluids includes liquids, air, and gases; therefore, *fluid dynamics* is an umbrella term that encompasses each of the specific subfields of hydrodynamics, aerodynamics, and gas dynamics. Since swimmers move through water, the more specific term that applies to swimming is *hydrodynamics,* but since fluid dynamics is the umbrella field, it is a suitable term as well.

been discussed and debated in the swimming community for decades. Having a basic grasp of the concepts in the following section will allow you to jump onto any swim forum that debates propulsion and contribute and, more important, will give you a valuable understanding of what propels you through the water.

## TWO TERMS EVERY SWIMMER SHOULD KNOW

Two ideas drive 90 percent of swim propulsion theory and discussion. These concepts are also fundamental to aerodynamics and flight. They are *drag* and *lift*.

Here are several ways to explain **drag**:

- Drag is the resistance a fluid has to being pushed aside.
- Drag is the force on an object that resists its motion through a fluid.
- Drag is a force that works parallel to the flow direction of a fluid (*parallel* here simply means "head-on").

Each of these definitions reinforces the idea that material things resist change to their velocity. They do not like to be moved, so they resist. This includes water. It will resist when a swimmer moves through it, and the resistance it puts up is called drag.

Most swimmers are familiar with how drag slows forward progress. Naturally, we want to feel as little head-on resistance/drag as possible as we stroke down the pool.

There are several types of drag; however, only one type—*form drag*—is addressed in this book, because it is the one that has the greatest effect on a swimmer's technique. (See the sidebar for the other type of drag that receives much attention in swimming but is unrelated to technique.)

Form drag refers to the size of the object moving through the fluid. A bigger object, with more surface area, will encounter more head-on resistance than a smaller object, with less surface area. This is why swimmers streamline off the walls—to make their "form" as low profile as possible and minimize drag.

Drag, then, is a simple enough concept. But keep a sharp mind. Note the explanation of drag as *working parallel to the flow direction* of a fluid. This becomes important once we talk about the second key concept: lift.

Also, do not assume that drag is only a negative force that hinders a swimmer's forward movement. In fact, it is quite the opposite. Drag is one of the best friends a swimmer has. Drag is a source of propulsion for a swimmer, and according to many, it is the dominant source of propulsion.

To understand how drag helps a swimmer move forward requires that Newton's Third Law enter the discussion. This law, in its simplest terms, states, "For every action there is an equal and opposite reaction."

Combining what we know about drag's resistive nature with Newton's Third Law, we get the following scenario: When a swimmer pushes back on the water with their limbs, the surface area (form) of the limbs will be subjected to the same parallel, head-on drag that impedes forward progress, but now the resistive force is beneficial; it allows the swimmer to push back against the water's resistance and in return move forward. It is Newton's Third Law in its most basic sense. The swimmer pushes back, and in return moves forward.

Thus, the term *drag* has different meanings in swimming, depending on the context. The term is used to describe forces that impede forward motion as well as forces that are a launching pad for forward motion. Once a swimmer is aware that the same word refers to both concepts, then the context in which the term is used indicates which drag is being referenced.

Figure 1.1 illustrates how drag can act as both a hindrance for a swimmer and a source of propulsion.

*Skin friction* is another type of drag that affects swimmers. As the name implies, it is the amount of resistance caused as fluid moves past the skin—or the surface—of an object. A rougher surface is subject to more skin friction than a smooth surface. Swimmers shave their body hair and wear tight suits to minimize skin friction.

**FIGURE 1.1.** Drag is a force that both impedes a swimmer and is a launching pad for propulsion.

Another key influence on swimming propulsion besides drag—and it's the only other option swimmers have if they want to get to the other end of the pool by their own accord—is **lift**.

The easiest way to understand lift is to consider an example with which we are all familiar: airplanes flying. This example will give us a visual image, and once we have an idea of how lift works on a plane, we can better visualize its role in the swim stroke.

An airplane gets off the ground because of a force called lift. The physics behind flying is quite complicated, but two basic conditions required for lift force can be applied to the swimming stroke. The first is the orientation, or angle, of the airplane wings. The wings are pitched up during takeoff. In physics this is called the *angle of attack*. For lift to occur there must be some angle/pitch to the wings.

The other condition required for lift is that there must be a pressure imbalance between the bottom of the wing and the top of the wing. The air pressure below the wing must be higher than the air pressure above the wing. Wings are designed such that air travels faster above the wing, causing lower pressure, and slower below the wing, causing higher pressure. The law that explains this correlation between air speed and pressure is called Bernoulli's Principle. It states that an increase in the speed of a fluid is always accompanied by a decrease in the pressure exerted by that fluid, and vice versa. We need not become experts in understanding the reasons behind this; we need only know that there must be more pressure on the bottom of the wing than on the top.

Now that the two basic conditions required for lift have been described, we can explain the lift force itself. Lift is the force that acts on the plane *perpendicular* to the direction of the oncoming flow of air, whereas drag is a force that acts *parallel* to the airflow.

To visualize, let's continue with our example of how airplanes get lift. As a plane picks up speed down a runway, air flows above and below the wings at different speeds, causing a buildup of higher pressure under the wings. Lift force starts once this pressure differential builds; lift begins to push up from under the wings. The upward force pressing on the underside of the wing is acting on the wing "perpendicular" to the direction that the plane (and air) is moving– air flows straight into the wings, and lift pushes up from the bottom side of the wing. The lift force, however, is too weak at this point to overcome the weight of the airplane; therefore, more lift is needed. This is where angle of attack enters the equation. The amount of lift force increases or decreases depending on the angle of attack. In order for lift force to overcome the weight of the plane, the wings must be pitched up more. The pilot uses controls to pull the nose of the plane up, and this positions the wings at an angle for more lift. Passengers on the plane feel this moment when the wings "grab" the air. It is a powerful force, and the plane soars off the ground.

How do lift forces relate to swimming? Swimmers create lift just as a plane does, but lift in swimming propels the swimmer forward, not up. Although the concept of lift implies an upward motion, the force can influence an object in any direction. Remember that lift acts perpendicular to the flow of the fluid, so lift force depends on which way the fluid flows past an object (or, conversely, which way the object moves through the fluid).

On an airplane we can easily imagine the direction the air takes as it passes by the wings, because the wings extend horizontally from the body of the plane.

A swimmer's hand/arm, however, which is likened to an airplane wing and therefore is the part of the body that generates lift force, is oriented vertically in the water during the propulsive phases of the stroke. This requires we use our imagination and visualize the rotated orientation. We must know which way the arm moves to know which way the fluid flows past the arm, and which way lift pushes.

The best way to understand how the arm moves in the swim stroke is to look at a popular drill in swimming called sculling. Sculling is specifically designed to teach a swimmer the sensation of propelling forward solely from lift force.

Figure 1.2 shows the drill in action. Sculling can be done in various positions, but this position in front of the swimmer's head is one of the most common.

In the sculling drill, the swimmer's hands/arms remain vertical as the swimmer sweeps the limbs out—away from each other—and then changes the hand/arm pitch to sweep them in toward each other. The limb, in its vertical position, pushes laterally against the water. There is no press backward; therefore, there is no forward movement from drag force. Drag acts laterally on the limbs, and the hand/arms pushing in opposite directions offset each other,

**FIGURE 1.2.** Sculling teaches swimmers the sensation of moving forward via lift force. Drag forces offset each other as the hands press laterally in opposite directions, but lift acts perpendicularly to push the swimmer forward.

preventing the swimmer from moving sideways. However, notice the pitch of the hand/arm (angle of attack) during the out-sweep and in-sweep phases, and notice that the palm side of the arm is the side that presses on the water during both sweeps, creating higher pressure on that side, as compared to the knuckle side. The pitch and the pressure meet our two requirements for lift in swimming. Lift acts perpendicularly to the lateral directing drag forces and pushes from the underside of the limb (the palm side) to give the swimmer a forward-directing push.

Anyone who has sculled before knows that it is not a drill that moves a swimmer quickly down the pool; it is a slow-moving drill. Therefore it may appear that lift is not a very powerful propulsive force in swimming. It is true that a swimmer would not win many races by sculling, but like most swimming drills, sculling is meant to isolate one characteristic of the stroke and exaggerate it to drive home a point. A sculling motion (any movement that is not back-pressing) as applied in an actual swim stroke can be incorporated with back-pressing (drag propulsion) stroking movements.

The combination of a parallel-acting drag force and a perpendicular-acting lift force yields a **resultant force**. A resultant force occurs when multiple forces acting on a body are reduced to one force. For example, if two people attempt to move a piece of furniture and one person pushes from one side and the other person from a slightly different angle, the two forces will yield a resultant force that moves the furniture in only one direction. If one person is stronger, their push will have more influence over which direction the furniture moves, but the other person's push did have influence too.

In an actual swim stroke the swimmer's hand/arm starts at a position extended in front of the head and ends at a position near the hips (the arms in breaststroke end in front of the chest), so back-pressing drag forces are undoubtedly in play. And since swimming is a three-dimensional sport, the swimmer can make skilled scull-like movements on a lateral or vertical plane that generate lift force. Drag and lift can coexist in a swim stroke, yielding a resultant force, as they do quite effectively in elite swimmers' strokes.

Figure 1.3 shows 200 IM world-record holder Ariana Kukors stroking during a very propulsive phase of the butterfly. As depicted by the arrows, drag and lift act in tandem to yield a single forward-directing resultant force. Notice the slight pitch (angle of attack) to her hand/forearm. She directs her hands/arms in (on the lateral plane), toward the midline of her body, as she presses back on the water during this phase of the stroke. This invites lift force on the scene alongside drag force. Without this pitch or "angle of attack," and the lateral (scull-like) movement, there is no lift force.

But *how much* force does Ariana generate by pushing back (drag) versus sweeping her hands/arms laterally in (lift) at this moment in the stroke? This is where the debate on propulsion begins.

Today, it is widely accepted that both drag and lift exist as forces in the swim stroke. The debate on propulsion centers on how much of a role each plays—or should play—in the stroking motion. Which dominates? Should a swimmer concentrate on pushing predominantly back on the water and generate mostly drag force, or exploit sculling motions and generate more lift force? The answer matters because it tells us how to best navigate our arms through the water.

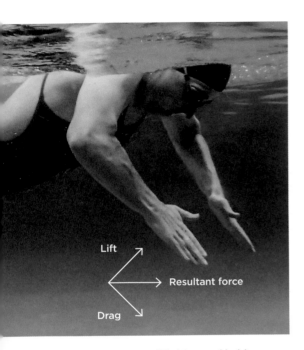

**FIGURE 1.3.** World-record holder Ariana Kukors propels herself down the pool in butterfly through a combination of drag and lift forces.

In the next section I discuss the theories of propulsion that have prevailed throughout recent decades, with the goal of inspiring you to look more closely at the photos in this book and notice details you may have otherwise not seen, such as hand pitch or stroking movement. Understanding the *why* of propulsion will positively influence your swim stroke.

# THEORIES OF PROPULSION

## DRAG IS EVERYTHING

Prior to the 1960s there was no question if drag (Newton's Third Law) was responsible for a swimmer's propulsion. It was agreed upon by all coaches that it was. The concept of lift as it could apply to swimming didn't even exist at the time. Coaches instructed their athletes to use their hand/arm like a paddle and push directly back on the water the entire length of the underwater stroke cycle. Any deviation from a straight path back was a fault in stroke technique as it veered the swimmer away from the fullest application of Newton's Third Law.

Stroking this way meant that a swimmer was operating solely on the fore/aft dimension of our three-dimensional sport. It told swimmers to ignore stroking laterally or vertically (sculling motions), because doing so pushed the body in directions other than forward. The rationale behind this instruction made sense.

There was only one problem with this theory—the best swimmers in the world were not doing it.

## DOC COUNSILMAN AND LIFT

James "Doc" Counsilman may not have turned the swimming world completely on its head, but he did turn it at least 90 degrees perpendicular when he introduced the concept of lift forces and their role in swimming propulsion in the early 1970s.

Doc was a famed swim coach at Indiana University who led his team to six NCAA Division I championships and served as the U.S. Men's head swim coach at the 1964 and 1976 Olympics. He also has the distinction of being the only coach in history whose swimmers held world records in every event at one time or another. Not just every stroke—*every event*. But his career had to start somewhere, in this case during the "Newtonian" era of swim theory in the late 1940s when he was a doctoral student and assistant swim coach at the University of Iowa.

While at Iowa in 1948 Doc devised a way to photograph the swim stroke underwater using a special underwater tank; one of his first film subjects was swimmer Walter Ris. Doc described what happened:

> *I photographed Walter Ris, the Olympic champion in the 100-meter free-*
> *style. He was pulling with a bent elbow with sort of an elliptical pull pat-*
> *tern. I changed him to a straight-arm pull and he slowed down. I said,*
> *"Something's wrong here." But I was pretty stupid. It took me 20 years to*
> *apply Bernoulli's Principle to it.* [*] *("Doc Counsilman," 2004)*

Doc's cameras kept rolling and evidence kept mounting that the best swimmers did not push straight back on the water as was being taught. Rather, they were stroking in a curvilinear path, incorporating lateral and vertical movements to the back-pushing stroke, just as Walter Ris had done.

In the early 1970s, 20 years after Doc's first suspicions were raised, he presented his findings to the swim community. Using photos of the underwater stroke patterns of current swim stars—many from his Indiana University team, including Mark Spitz—Doc showed the curvilinear pull patterns (in all strokes) and offered an explanation as to why the best swimmers were stroking this way.

Doc first explained the limitations of Newton's Third Law as it applied to swimming. He said that when a swimmer exerts a back-pushing force on the water, the water begins to move, and once the water is set in motion it offers less resistance to the swimmer. Doc explained the swimmer's hand/arm would have to continually accelerate to keep up with the moving water. Accelerating in this manner, stroke after stroke, would be exhausting and an inefficient use of the swimmer's energy.

Doc believed that Newton's Third Law was effective for pushing water back in short increments but not longer increments such as the full length of the underwater stroke. He believed that by moving the hand/arm to an adjacent

---

[*] Remember, Bernoulli's Principle cites the correlation between air speed and pressure and is one of the laws in physics used to explain lift force on airplanes.

plane of water either to the side, below, or above the backward-directing path, the swimmer would find slower-moving or "still" water and could effectively apply Newton's Third Law again.

This part of Doc's explanation was easy for coaches to accept since it preserved most of the commonly held action-reaction beliefs of the time; however, the second part of Doc's presentation caused a stir. He explained that the lateral and vertical stroking patterns were not just a necessary evil for the swimmer to maneuver their way to a plane of still water, but rather that propulsive power was actually generated by these movements—perhaps even more propulsive power than drag could offer. Doc then explained Bernoulli's Principle and introduced the concept of lift to the swimming world for the first time in the sport's history. His first published article on the topic was "The Application of Bernoulli's Principle to Human Propulsion in Water" (1970).

Doc's theory became known in swimming circles as the *S-Pull pattern*. He explained that just as a boat driven by a propeller is faster than a boat driven by a paddle, so too is a swimmer who navigates the hands/arms like a propeller (in an S-curve path) through the water faster than a swimmer who uses the hands/arms like a paddle pushing straight back.

Doc's discovery swung the pendulum. The drag-dominated theory of the pre-1960s was out, and his lift-dominated theory took over. The 1970s were a decade of great change for swimming. Swimmers began incorporating scull-like movements on the lateral and vertical dimensions alongside their back-pressing stroking motions.

## CECIL COLWIN AND VORTICES

Doc Counsilman's introduction of lift force did more than just influence stroking habits worldwide; he was the first to show that science played a significant role in understanding and coaching swimming technique. His book *The Science of Swimming* (1968) ignited an interest in fluid dynamics, and a wave of research, that continues to this day.

Cecil Colwin was one of those inspired. He was Doc's peer in the Southern Hemisphere whose swimmers in South Africa were breaking world records and winning Olympic medals in the 1950s and 1960s. Cecil dove headlong into his own research. He agreed with Doc that swimmers should not press straight back on the water but instead take a curved path back, and he followed Doc's lead on lift propulsion; however, he was not convinced by one part of Doc's lift theory explanation: Whereas airplanes and propellers produce lift in a steady fluid-flow environment (wings are attached in a fixed position on an airplane, and propeller blades are welded at a fixed angle of attack, so air flows steadily past), the hands/arms of swimmers constantly change direction and operate in an unsteady fluid-flow environment. Cecil felt that lift could not be generated in the same manner for swimmers as it was for fixed wings or propellers on airplanes.

Cecil's curiosity to learn how lift is generated in environments of unsteady fluid flow led him to research the wing actions of birds and insects and the flipper actions of marine mammals. He concluded, like Doc, that lift was the dominant force in swimming propulsion, but that it was created in a manner similar to that found in nature's flight rather than in engineered flight. Cecil explained that as wings of a bird oscillate/pitch, pressure differentials build and start air circulating around the wing. The circulation creates a *vortex*—fluid that rotates around an axis—and it is this vortex circulation, superimposed on the general fluid flow, that is the lift-generating (propulsion-generating) mechanism.

Cecil said that the lateral and transverse stroking movements of swimmer's hands/forearms cause a pressure differential that starts flow circulation around the hand/forearm like that on an oscillating wing. The circulation "wraps" or "swirls" around the limb, forming a vortex that generates lift force/propulsion.

Cecil coached his swimmers to become skilled "shapers of the flow," explaining that every time the hand makes a directional change to an adjacent plane of water, the existing vortex that was bound around the limb is shed, and a new one quickly formed. He warned that the vortices should not be shed too quickly or randomly, as this is a sign of wasted energy. Vortices are visible when a swimmer travels at top speeds and entraps air into the stroke. Cecil could see, based on the shed vortices left in the water behind the stroking motion, if a swimmer was efficient or not. Prematurely shed vortices were a sign to him that the swimmer's hand/wrist was too rigid, or that the swimmer made a directional change too quickly. Cecil also pointed out that vortices form around the feet during the kicking action and are shed at the finish of the kick.

In sum, while Cecil agreed with Doc on the mechanics of the stroke (the curved pull path), he encouraged swimmers to be sensitive to flow circulations and not become "mechanical" in their stroking actions. Don't take your cue from the propeller blade or airplane wing, he might say; take it from nature, and feel the flow.

## ERNIE MAGLISCHO AND DRAG

Cecil Colwin and Doc Counsilman both asserted that swimming propulsion is dominated by lift forces, albeit by different reasonings (Doc—Bernoulli's Principle; Cecil—vortices). Ernie Maglischo—reknowned collegiate swimming coach whose teams won 13 NCAA Division II Championship titles, and who holds a PhD in exercise physiology—believed lift was dominant, too—at least for a while. Underwater review of the stroking motions of elite swimmers showed that their hands/arms appeared to move more on the lateral and vertical dimensions than the fore-aft dimension, so there could be no explanation other than lift-force domination. Ernie published books in line with Doc's viewpoint, focusing on Bernoulli's Principle and the precise hand angles of attack that are crucial during the propeller-blade movements to maximize lift propulsion in each of the swimming strokes.

As research continued in the 1990s, however, two findings cast a shadow over the soundness of Bernoulli's Principle and lift-dominated propulsion. First, it was brought to light that Bernoulli's Principle was not applicable to human swimming propulsion, because a swimmer's hand/arm is neither contoured properly nor smooth enough (as is a wing/propeller) to sustain a boundary layer over its surface. A boundary layer is a thin layer of fluid that is in contact with the surface of the object over which the fluid flows, and it is a requisite of Bernoulli's Principle. On a swimmer's hand/arm the boundary layer separates. At the same time Bernoulli's role in swimming propulsion was under scrutiny, more sophisticated studies (computer simulations, and plaster hand models held against fluid flow at varying angles of attack) were conducted that showed drag forces were dominant throughout the swim stroke, not lift.

Ernie went back to the drawing board to reexamine his research and conclusions. First he looked closely at the S-pull path. How necessary was it if Bernoulli's Principle could no longer explain lift in the swim stroke, and if drag appeared to dominate propulsion? Should swimmers focus more on pushing straight back? While studying the pull path, Ernie found, like Doc, that swimmers could apply propulsive force more effectively if they navigated away from moving water and onto an adjacent plane of "still" water. He also cited that a curved path back is longer than a straight path back, and longer is better, because swimmers can apply propulsive force over more distance and for a longer period of time on each stroke cycle.

Once he determined the curved path had warranted benefits, Ernie set out to examine the new research results—which showed drag to be dominant—and what these results meant for how a swimmer should specifically navigate the hands/arms to adjacent planes of water. If drag was dominant, which Ernie now believed was the case based on the research findings, then swimmers need not worry about the precise hand/arm angles of attack that maximize lift force. They should rather focus more on pressing back, and utilize lift and pitch only to the extent that they direct the hand/arm through a longer path and onto adjacent planes of water where drag force can be more effectively applied. (Note: Although Bernoulli's Principle was no longer applicable to swimming, Ernie explained that lift can, and does, exist in the stroke: Swimmers create the necessary pressure differential simply by pressing on the water with the palm-side of the hand/arm, creating more pressure on that side than the knuckle side.) In *Swimming Fastest* (2003), Ernie explains why measuring lift and drag, and understanding which force is dominant, is so important:

> *Swimmers propel themselves with a combination of lift and drag forces. You might wonder why it is important to know which of the two forces, lift or drag, makes the greater contribution. It is because the force that*

*contributes the most determines the emphasis of propulsive movement. If lift forces make the great contribution, swimmers should execute large lateral and vertical propeller-like sweeps with the limbs and those sweeps should have a minimal backward component. Conversely, if the contribution of drag force is greater, as I believe it is, swimmers should put their effort into pushing the limbs back against the water during the propulsive phases of their strokes. (Maglischo 2003, 22)*

His research made it plain to Ernie that swimmers should focus their efforts on the fore-aft dimension, but he clarified that this does not mean swimmers should return to the straight-back path of the 1960s. The curved path is important. He writes, "Swimmers do not push the arms straight back through the water. Rather, they seem to push back against the water as they stroke diagonally through it" (Maglischo 2003, 33).

Ernie explains in his book that the amount of force generated by a diagonal stroking motion is slightly less than if a swimmer faces the hand/arm 100 percent back and pushes 100 percent back on the water, but the reduction is negligible and more than made up for by the longer stroking path. Furthermore, he said, stroking directly back would require athletes to maintain high rates of turnover (to keep up with the moving water), which is inefficient.

Through decades-long study and passion for getting to the heart of propulsion, Ernie concluded that swimmers should press predominantly back as they take a curved, or diagonal, path through the water.

—

The four theories of propulsion presented in this chapter have prevailed at one point or another throughout the decades. Two of them stand strong today—Cecil Colwin's vortex theory and Ernie Maglischo's drag theory. While Cecil and Ernie are on different ends of the lift/drag spectrum in terms of which force is the dominating propulsive mechanism, they do not differ on the matter that is most important for swimmers to note and deliberately train—the curved path through the water.

The following chapters are filled with photos showing the underwater stroking motions of elite swimmers. I hope the science inspires you to look closely at hand/arm positions and angles, and the stroking path, understanding that the laws of physics are at play in the deep blue, and your stroking motion depends on these.

# 2

## THE LOOK AND FEEL OF LIFT AND DRAG

**LIFT AND DRAG WERE INTRODUCED** in the previous chapter to make swimmers aware of their very real presence in our sport. It is no exaggeration to say that these two concepts define competitive swimming. Without them we are just floaters. But knowing of them is only the start. Now it is time to understand what they look like in the swim stroke. Just as important, it is time to learn what they feel like.

To know what these forces look like requires studying the patterns and characteristics of a stroke's propulsive components—the arm pull and kick. This chapter focuses on the pull, as it is the most complex component of the strokes. The kick, also a valuable source of propulsion, will be addressed in the next chapter along with the other major component of the stroke—the core movement.

We will look at the pull of the four strokes side by side in this chapter before moving on to the stroke-specific chapters later in the book. By showing the strokes alongside each other, the notable traits of propulsion become evident. While butterfly, backstroke, breaststroke, and freestyle are recognizably unique when observed from above the water, they share the same propulsive characteristics underwater. They must, since they are all crafted from lift and drag forces.

To know what lift and drag feel like requires visiting a more abstract topic known as a "feel" for the water. Describing feel can get so abstract that coaches are oftentimes heard commenting that the greatest swimmers look as "one with the water." The best seem to have an "X factor" working in their favor. Their strokes are fluid and look effortless. We will end the chapter by defining the X factor. The X is not abstract, nor is it a gift handed out by fate. It can be learned. Our study of fluid dynamics and stroke mechanics reveals what swimmers must do to add the X factor in their strokes.

## THE PULL

Developing a mechanically sound pull in swimming demands more concentration than any other part of the stroke. It is the only component that requires coordinated movements on all three dimensions—lateral, vertical, and fore/aft. The other parts of the strokes—the kick and the core movement—require that the swimmer work in two dimensions only. This is not to say that functioning on two dimensions is easy, especially considering that everything has to be coordinated into a whole stroke. It just means that the pull adds more than its fair share to overall swimming demands. (Note: The breaststroke kick is three-dimensional, but it will get its own special attention in the breaststroke chapter.)

### THE CURVILINEAR PATH

To begin understanding the pull we must visit the concept that was referred to in the theories of propulsion as a "curvilinear" path, also described as "a predominantly backward-directing path with diagonal components." Although the theories differ as to whether the pull is lift or drag dominated, they are in full agreement (post-1960s) that elite swimmers do not push straight back on the water but rather take a curved path back. The best swimmers utilize all three dimensions available to them as they stroke.

To review, a curvilinear path is beneficial for two reasons:

- It allows the swimmer to navigate away from moving water and onto an adjacent plane of "still" water where force is more effectively applied.

- It allows a swimmer to apply propulsive force over more distance and for a longer period of time on each stroke, because the hand/arm travels a longer path through the water than it would taking a straight path back.

What does it look like to move the hand/arm onto a nearby plane of still water, and to take a longer stroking path while pushing back? The following figures are examples from each of the four strokes that showcase this curvilinear or back-directing diagonal path.

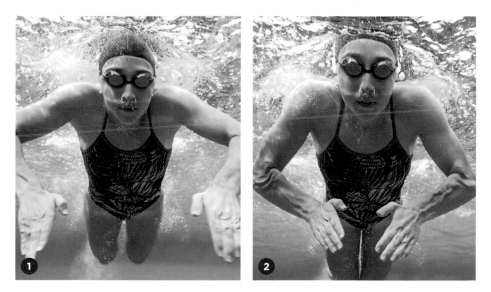

**FIGURE 2.1.** Ariana Kukors sweeps her hands/arms in as she presses back during the butterfly pull. Note the pressure against her forearms in Frame 2. As she moves onto an adjacent plane of water, lengthening her propulsive stroking path, she does not lose her connection with lift and drag forces.

**FIGURE 2.2.** World-record holder Aaron Peirsol sweeps his hand/arm up to an adjacent plane of water during his backstroke pull. Note that Aaron's hand/arm faces back on the water in both frames. The hands/arms of elite swimmers face predominantly back, and press back, throughout the pull cycle, even as they navigate to adjacent planes of water.

**FIGURE 2.3.** World-record holder Rebecca Soni sweeps her hands/arms up and in as she presses back on the water during the breaststroke pull. She utilizes all three dimensions in the deep blue to propel herself forward.

**FIGURE 2.4.** Olympic gold medalist Peter Vanderkaay sweeps his hand under his body, taking a curved—rather than straight—path back in freestyle. Notice that his hand/arm faces back on the water in both frames.

## THE THREE PHASES OF THE PULL

In every stroke, world-class swimmers utilize the three dimensions available to them underwater. They navigate a *curved path back*. The question then becomes, "How many curves or directional changes do they make on each stroke?"

Elite swimmers make two directional changes during the underwater pull. Two is plenty. Water will resist us for a time before it courteously moves out of our way, and we are better served by finding a nearby column that will resist us again. (Note that breaststroke has only one propulsive directional change because the hands/arms do not pull back to the hips.)

The directional changes occur at specific points during the underwater stroke cycle. The first change occurs approximately one-third of the way into the stroke, and the second change happens approximately two-thirds into the stroke. By noting where the directional changes occur, we can divide the pull into three phases and study the characteristics of each (breaststroke includes only the first two phases). Although I call these *phases,* do not think of the pull as three separate motions. The arm pull is a fluid motion, and directional changes are slight and blend in seamlessly.

The three underwater propulsive phases are the catch, the diagonal, and the finish.*

## THE CATCH PHASE

The catch is the first moment in each stroke cycle when a swimmer has positioned the hands/arms to face back in the water so as to utilize lift and drag force in a forward-directing manner. It deserves special attention because of the challenging position the swimmer is in while maneuvering to the back-facing position. The catch is the only propulsive phase of the stroke cycle that takes place overhead.

A good catch requires resiliency and strength. Elite swimmers who have already developed a championship catch never go a day in training without maintaining or building on this part of the stroke. It too easily slips away without regular attention.

To set up for the catch, a swimmer transitions to the overhead position by extending the arms in the water after they have recovered forward from the finish of the previous stroke cycle.

To extend the arms overhead, a swimmer works from the muscles in the upper back to press the scapula (the shoulder blade) forward. Figure 2.5 shows the muscles that surround the scapula working as Peter Vanderkaay extends and catches in freestyle.

To transition from the nonpropulsive extension in Frame 1 to the propulsive (back-facing) bent-arm catch position in Frame 2, a swimmer must attend to three vital details: medially rotate the upper arm, sweep the upper arm outside of shoulder width, and gradually bend the elbow. Let's examine each detail more closely.

---

* The nonpropulsive phases of each stroke—entry of the hands/arms into the water to start a new stroke cycle, and recovery of the hands/arms forward after finishing the pull cycle—will be addressed in the individual stroke chapters.

**FIGURE 2.5.** Peter presses his scapula forward from the extension (1) through to the catch (2). His propulsive path is lengthened when he positions his hand/arm facing back on the water while still overhead, as in Frame 2.

Medial rotation is a twisting of the upper arm, wherein a swimmer rotates the arm to direct the elbow slightly *up* (in backstroke the elbow directs forward). Deftly directing the elbow this way is key to establishing what is termed in swimming "the high-elbow catch." A high elbow does not refer as much to the actual height of the elbow in the water as it does the upward-directing (forward-directing in backstroke) orientation of the joint. You can see that the bony tip of Peter's elbow points to the side of the pool in Frame 1 while he extends, and it directs up in Frame 2 during his catch. Medial rotation is important because it activates the powerful lat muscles in the back.

Swimmers must also sweep the upper arm wide of shoulder width while transitioning from the straight-arm extension to the bent-elbow catch. When

When training the catch, sweep your upper arms outside shoulder width only to where you feel strong and coordinated and to where there is no strain on the shoulder joint. Use elite swimmers as a guide, but ultimately determine the width of your catch based on what feels mechanically sound to you.

the upper arm is set wide of the shoulder, a swimmer is in a mechanically strong position to handle the forces of lift and drag. The degree to which a swimmer sweeps the upper arms outside the shoulders varies by stroke as well as individual preference. The goal when determining the best width is to position where the arms and upper back muscles feel strongest and most coordinated, and where there is no strain on the shoulder joint.

Finally, the most noticeable feature of the catch is the bent-arm position. While sweeping wide of shoulder width and medially rotating the upper arm, the swimmer *gradually* (not abruptly) bends the arm at the elbow; this positions the limb vertically and facing back on the water to make the catch.

The catch demands a great deal of concentration and agility, as well as a unique strength to operate the scapula and upper arm in ways that don't simulate anything even vaguely familiar in everyday life, but it is quite manageable if practiced deliberately and regularly. Following is a summary of the four ingredients required for a beautiful catch in all strokes:

- The scapula actively presses the arm forward (overhead).
- The upper arm medially rotates to direct the elbow slightly up (forward in backstroke).
- The upper arm sweeps some degree wide of shoulder width.
- The arm gradually bends at the elbow.

The following photos show Olympic swimmers moving from extension to the catch in each stroke. The similarities from stroke to stroke are remarkable.

**FIGURE 2.6.** Ariana presses her scapula forward as she extends (1) and catches (2) in butterfly. The farther overhead she can position her hands/forearms facing back on the water, the longer her propulsive stroking path.

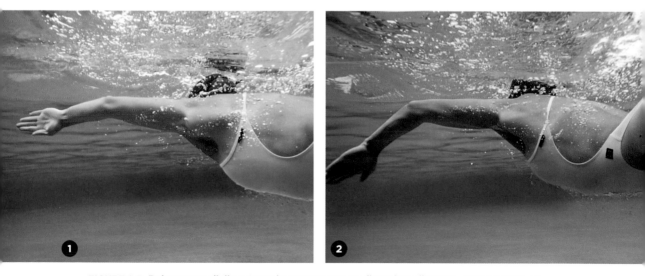

**FIGURE 2.7.** Rebecca medially rotates her upper arm to direct her elbow up, sweeps wide of shoulder width, and bends her elbows as she makes the catch overhead (2) in breaststroke.

**FIGURE 2.8.** Gold medalist Ashley Whitney extends (1) and then medially rotates her elbow up to make the catch (2) in freestyle. Her propulsive path is lengthened because her hand/forearm faces back on the water while still overhead.

Backstrokers swim in a supine position, so the catch looks different than it does in other strokes. The arm is horizontal as the catch is made, and medial rotation directs the elbow forward rather than toward the water surface. Although it looks different, the ingredients required for a great overhead catch are the same. Figure 2.9 shows Aaron Peirsol extending in Frame 1 and catching in Frame 2. Aaron is taking a breakout stroke in these photos (the breakout stroke is the first pull that brings a swimmer to the surface after pushing off the wall and streamlining underwater). Swimmers should always establish great form on the breakout stroke, as this sets the tone for all strokes the rest of the length of the pool.

The strength, resiliency, and patience to feel for the catch is not perfected in one session, but it is a skill that any swimmer can build over time with thoughtful and deliberate practice. You will have more success at mastering the four

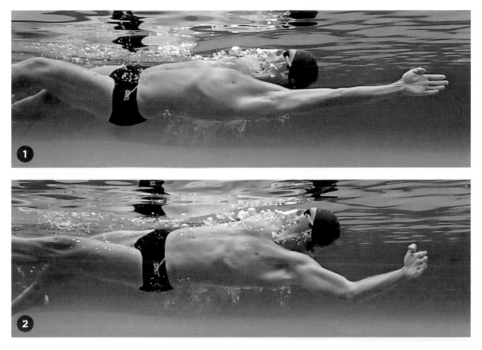

**FIGURE 2.9.** Aaron extends (1) and then medially rotates his upper arm, which directs his elbow forward (the direction he is moving), to make the catch (2). By continuously pressing his scapula forward as he bends his elbow, he makes the catch (hand/forearm facing back on the water) while his arm is still overhead.

ingredients if you slow down and concentrate on each detail, one at a time. Swim easy. Roll into the catch position slowly and gently. Elite swimmers train this way often. When you want to go fast, you must fire into these positions more aggressively and quickly, but you will only be able to do so if you first take a few steps back and master the details patiently.

Also remember, if you consider yourself a one-stroke specialist, training the catch in all strokes helps you strengthen the catch for your primary stroke because of the propulsive similarities.

## THE DIAGONAL PHASE

Once a swimmer makes the catch and begins to press back on the water, it is not long before it's time to make the first directional change to the diagonal phase of the stroke. This change is made when the hands/arms are still slightly overhead or just passing by/under the swimmer's head.

I call this phase the "diagonal," because when swimmers navigate the directional change correctly, both the lower and upper arms position at 45-degree angles in relation to the water surface. Figure 2.10 shows this trademark fea-

**FIGURE 2.10.** During the diagonal phase of the stroke, the lower and upper arms position at a 45-degree angle in relation to the water's surface. There is also a 90-degree bend in the elbow.

ture in butterfly, backstroke, breaststroke, and freestyle. Notice also the 90-degree elbow bend in each stroke.

To come to the strong diagonal position we see in Figure 2.10, swimmers must do two things while pressing back on the water: Release the medial rotation in the upper arm, and press the hand/forearm slightly up and in, onto an adjacent plane of water. This phase of the stroke requires coordinated movement from both the upper arm and hand/forearm—of *equal magnitude*. Some swimmers make the mistake of pressing significantly more with their hand during this phase of the stroke, leaving the elbow trailing behind, while others drop the elbow back on the fore-aft dimension, leaving the hand/forearm trailing and slipping through the water.

In addition to achieving those desired 45-degree angles, other signs that you are navigating the diagonal phase correctly are that your elbow now points out rather than up (in backstroke it points down during the diagonal), and your hand and forearm align as one giant paddle.

Let's look at how elite swimmers transition from the catch to the diagonal in all four strokes. Just as with the catch, the similarities are remarkable.

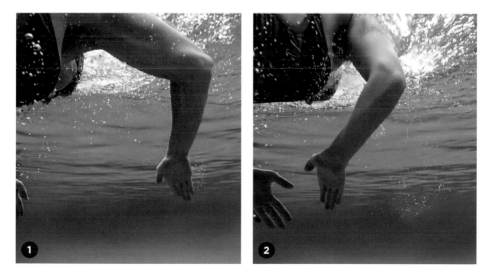

**FIGURE 2.11.** Ariana transitions from the catch (1) to the diagonal phase of the stroke (2) in butterfly. Her hands/forearms align as giant paddles as she presses back on the water.

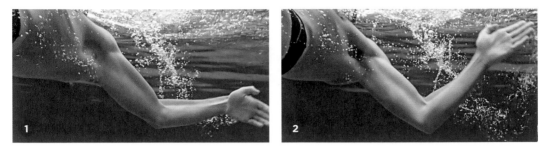

**FIGURE 2.12.** Aaron presses back and directs his hand/forearm up and in as he moves from the catch (1) to the diagonal (2).

**FIGURE 2.13.** Rebecca's elbows direct up during the catch (1) and out during the diagonal (2) in breaststroke. She continually presses back as she sweeps her hands/forearms up and in.

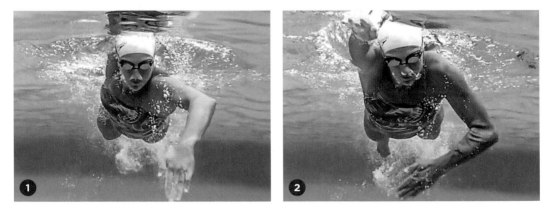

**FIGURE 2.14.** Ashley medially rotates her upper arm during the catch (1), and releases the rotation for the diagonal phase of the stroke (2).

The diagonal phase of the stroke is not as mechanically awkward and challenging a position as the catch, but it must be navigated correctly to generate full power. Just as with the catch, diligently training the details of the diagonal in any stroke strengthens your primary stroke because of the propulsive similarities across the board during this phase.

## THE FINISH PHASE

Once a swimmer's hand/forearm passes by the ribcage, it is time to make the second and final directional change to finish the underwater pull (in all strokes except breaststroke, which concludes with the diagonal phase and then recovers the arms forward). In each of the three strokes that have a finish phase—butterfly, backstroke, and freestyle—the hand makes a directional change to lengthen the stroking path and move the limb to an adjacent plane of water, shown in the following photos.

**FIGURE 2.15.** Ariana transitions from the diagonal phase of the butterfly pull (1) to the finish phase (2) by skillfully adjusting the pitch of her hands. She continues to press back on the water as she makes the directional change.

**FIGURE 2.16.** Aaron transitions from the diagonal (1) to the finish (2) in backstroke by pitching his hand slightly down and out as he presses back.

**FIGURE 2.17.** Ashley adjusts the pitch of her right hand as she transitions from the diagonal phase (1) to the finish phase (2) in freestyle.

There are nuances to the finish phase that are particular to each stroke; these will be discussed in the stroke-specific chapters. The commonality among the three strokes, however, as shown here, is the all-important directional change that occurs. The hand pitch adjustment directs the propulsive limb onto an adjacent plane of water and lengthens the stroking path back.

## THE X FACTOR IN SWIMMING: A FEEL FOR THE WATER

Our review of the curvilinear pull reveals that elite swimmers are astute technicians. The same stroking mechanics show up time and time again in Olympic gold medalists' and world-record holders' strokes, no matter which athlete or which stroke we study. But is precise technique the final answer, or is there something more? What makes them look fluid and almost effortless when they swim? What is the "X factor" that exists in their strokes?

That X factor involves what in swimming is called a *feel* for the water. Feel is also referred to as an athlete's "hold" on the water—the ability to gain traction on a fluid and translate it into forward movement. We all are subject to lift and drag in the water. How do elite swimmers feel when they interact with these forces? Do they feel them like everyone else, or do they have a different, gifted, sensory function?

Elite swimmers do *not* feel lift and drag differently. Lift and drag are simply felt as resistance or pressure on the limb. You can press your hand/arm in any direction on the water and feel the resistance. There is no secret to it. However, elite swimmers do have sharpened kinesthetic and proprioceptive abilities, which allow them to feel how the force they exert against the resistance translates to speed in the water, as well as when the resistance can be used to propel themselves forward.

*Kinesthesia* is the ability to feel movements of the limbs and the body, and *proprioception* is the ability to sense the position and location of the body and its parts. These two sensory skills account for the fluidity and almost effortless-looking nature of elite swimmers' strokes. Having kinesthetic and proprioceptive abilities may be a gift that some swimmers naturally have, but these can be developed in any athlete through deliberate practice. Let's look at what swimmers must do to develop these heightened abilities, so they can put the X factor in their strokes.

## KINESTHETIC ABILITY

Developing kinesthetic ability requires that swimmers do two things while navigating the curvilinear pull path: Maximize the surface area of the limb that comes in contact with the water, and hold the proper amount of muscle tension in the limb (not too rigid; not too relaxed).

The more surface area presented to the oncoming flow of water, the more you will feel, and be able to press against, or "hold," the water. If you have ever done the fist swimming drill (a drill where you close your hands in a fist rather than open them while stroking) then you know that there is much more feel or "hold" on the water when the hand is held flat as opposed to the fist position. In every photo in this book you will see that elite swimmers hold their hands flat to maximize surface area. You will also see that their wrist is straight, which keeps the forearm in line with the hand, creating a large stroking paddle. Figure 2.18 shows that Peter strokes with his hand flat and his wrist straight. His hand/forearm form one large stroking paddle.

**FIGURE 2.18.** Peter feels the pressure against his hand/forearm and uses it to propel himself forward.

Also note the muscle tone in Peter's stroking hand and arm. He holds strong against the water's resistance, but he is not rigid. A rigid muscle cannot feel sensations, such as water pressure, well, and a relaxed muscle will not be able to resist the forces. When you stroke, find the right tone, and train muscle endurance to maintain the tone stroke after stroke. Notice that most elite swimmers press back on the water with their fingers held together, but not tightly. In some photos you will see a very slight spacing between the fingers. Study the specifics of hand/arm tone and finger spacing in the photos throughout the book, as this is an important stroking feature that pertains to your feel for the water.

## PROPRIOCEPTIVE ABILITY

It won't do you much good to develop kinesthetic abilities only to then press on the water in the wrong direction. Your hand/arm must face back on the water throughout the curvilinear path in such a way that the resultant forces of lift and drag propel you forward. Hav-

ing the proprioceptive ability to recognize when your limb is in the correct position is critical.

In Figure 2.19, Vladimir Morozov knows exactly the orientation of his hand/fore-arm paddle as he finishes the stroke in freestyle. He cannot see that his limb is positioned facing back on the water, but he knows it is so because he feels a recogniz-able resistance from the water that can be used to propel him forward.

When you train, take time occasion-ally to stop swimming midstroke, freeze-frame your hand/arm during the pull, and look back to see if your stroking paddle faces back on the water. If not, adjust the orientation/pitch, and consciously work to memorize what it feels like.

**FIGURE 2.19.** Vladimir Morozov, finishing the stroke in freestyle, feels that his hand and forearm face back in the water although he cannot see the limb.

## THE OTHER INGREDIENT TO FEEL—HAND SPEED

When it comes to a masterful hold on the water, there is one other stroking feature that elite swimmers share: hand acceleration. Elite swimmers' hand speed is slowest during the catch and increases as they progress through the stroke, while less proficient swimmers stroke with constant, unchanging hand velocity. Hand speed is directly related to hand force; faster hand speed translates to increased force. Therefore, elite swimmers' hand force increases as they progress through the stroke cycle.

Don't rush and try to muscle the water back during the catch. Patiently position the limb to face back, so that lift and drag are usable in a forward-directing manner, and apply force thoughtfully. Once you make the directional change to the diagonal (which comes up soon enough), hand speed—hence, hand force—should gradually increase as you progress to the finish phase of the pull. (Note: Velocity dips slightly during the directional change to the finish phase; however, there is an overall increase from midstroke to finish.) Elite swimmers accelerate the mass of water they feel on their hand/arm backward at the finish of the stroke, and then immediately release (let go of) the water to lift for the recovery.

Seasoned coaches oftentimes call stroking motions *impulses.* An impulse is a change in momentum. Feel how the resistance on your limbs, and your varying hand speed, translates to momentum in your stroke.

Another definition for *impulse* is "a strong and unreflective urge or desire to act." When you feel resistance on your limbs you should feel a desire to move forward, and sense how this is done effectively. Let's end the chapter by looking at Figure 2.20, where you can almost see Elizabeth Beisel's urge to act against the resistance she feels on her hands/forearms. She looks forward. She's thinks, *Forward.* She knows exactly how to use lift and drag to go forward.

I hope you just felt an impulse to get to the pool and work on your stroke!

**FIGURE 2.20.** Olympic medalist Elizabeth Beisel feels lift and drag on her hands/forearms and knows how to use them to propel herself powerfully down the pool.

# 3

## THE KICK, CORE MOVEMENT, AND CONNECTION

**AS WE SAW IN THE PREVIOUS** chapter, a properly navigated pull path has many facets. It is Olympic-level athleticism and proprioception in three dimensions. However, if broken down into small pieces and deliberately practiced, it can be mastered by anyone. It is important to spend time dialing in the path not just for the sake of having a strong and effective pull, but also because it is critical to the overall function of the stroke. Swimmers who want to realize their full potential must synch the pull with the other two major components in the swim stroke—the kick and core movement. If the pull path is off, then the rest of the stroke will be off too.

In this chapter we will learn about that connection. The fastest speeds reached by a swimmer occur when all components work like cogs in a gear train. Everything turns and connects in time.

Before looking at how the components of the strokes connect, we will study the kick and core movement separately. The kick—like the pull—is a source of propulsion for a swimmer. It makes use of lift and drag forces to generate forward movement. The core—or trunk of the body—cannot face back on the water and press against lift and drag forces like the arms and legs can; therefore, it cannot generate propulsion. As far as its relationship with fluid flow, it can only experience the "bad drag" that was explained in Chapter 1. This doesn't mean it merely gets dragged along for the ride, however. Rather, the core plays a major role in the swim strokes. Indeed, many elite swimmers feel that their mastery of the core's function is what separates them from the field.

## THE KICK

Kicking is such a powerful source of propulsion when a swimmer employs proper technique that in many instances, athletes are faster kicking underwater than they are stroking at the surface. This is partly because there is more turbulence at the surface than down in the deep blue, but it is also because lift and drag can be utilized so effectively on the powerful lower limbs.

Swimmers and coaches realized the propulsive potential of the legs in the 1980s, and in a short-lived era of swimming history—from 1988 to 1998—spectators never knew if they would witness a race swum on the surface of the water or underwater. Athletes who mastered the underwater kick submarined off the start, and they, along with everyone else in the natatorium, held their breath until they popped to the surface 25–35 meters later. It was exciting, oddly spectator friendly and unfriendly at the same time, and indisputably dangerous. Athletes were pushing the limits by holding their breath off the starts and turns. The rule books were changed immediately for backstroke in 1988, and then in 1998 for butterfly and freestyle, mandating that swimmers surface by the 15-meter mark off the starts and turns (there is no such rule for breaststroke, because swimmers are limited to one underwater pull and kick).

The kick is undoubtedly a powerful weapon if used off the walls to its full potential (more explanation in upcoming chapters), but what happens when it is combined with the arm pull and core movement for a full stroke? How much does it contribute to overall speed? In this section we will examine kicking technique, and in an upcoming section we will study timing the kick within the stroke so as to maximize its contribution to overall speed.

## KICKING TECHNIQUE

In each of the four strokes the goal of the kick is like that of the arm pull: to establish a back-facing position with the limbs so that propulsive forces can be used to direct the swimmer forward. While the entire leg is involved in the kicking action, the feet are the swimmer's connection to lift and drag forces. In butterfly, backstroke, and freestyle, a swimmer connects with lift and drag on the *tops* of the feet. Breaststroke is the lone-wolf stroke when it comes to kicking; technical rules state, "The feet must be turned outward during the propulsive part of the kick." In other words, no pointing of the feet is allowed (during propulsion); thus swimmers in breaststroke have no other choice than to connect with lift and drag on the *bottoms* of the feet.

To establish a powerful back-facing position with the feet, swimmers in all strokes must bend the leg at the knee before the propulsive phase of the kick. Figure 3.1 shows the bent-knee position in each of the strokes. Vladimir Morozov bends in freestyle (right leg), Aaron Peirsol in backstroke (left leg), Elizabeth Beisel in butterfly, and Laura Sogar in breaststroke.

**FIGURE 3.1.** In all strokes, swimmers must bend at the knee to establish a back-facing position with the feet before the propulsive phase of the kick.

In butterfly, backstroke, and freestyle, elite swimmers also pigeon-toe the feet (turn them in) to gain extra range of motion in the ankle joint. This gives the swimmer an even better back-facing position, and more surface area for feeling the water's resistance with the feet. We see the pigeon-toe position (big toes pointing toward each other) in Figure 3.2 as Doug Reynolds demonstrates an underwater butterfly/dolphin kick.

**FIGURE 3.2.** Elite butterflyer Doug Reynolds pigeon-toes to gain extra range of motion in the ankle joint and a better back-facing position with his feet.

Kicking in all strokes except breaststroke is a two-dimensional movement. To generate propulsion, freestylers and butterflyers kick *back* and *down* from the bent-knee position, straightening the leg in the process. Since backstrokers are in a supine position, the propulsive phase of the kick is *back* and *up*.

The kicking action starts in the hip before traveling through the leg. The swimmer presses the upper leg slightly down (up in backstroke), which flexes the powerful hip. Hip flexion can be seen in each of the photos in Figure 3.1. Starting the kick in this manner generates power that will travel the length of the leg as the swimmer extends the lower leg *back* and *down* (*back* and *up* in backstroke). It is a wave-like or whip-like action. The leg straightens completely by the end of the kick, and the swimmer *maintains the straight-leg position* while recovering the limb *up* (*down* in backstroke) for the next propulsive kick. During the straight-leg recovery phase, hip flexion returns to neutral.

Figure 3.3 shows Vladimir kicking freestyle underwater. Focus on his right leg as we review the kick technique. In Frame 1 Vladimir bends his knee to face his foot back on the water. He initiates the kicking action by flexing his hip (pressing his thigh down slightly) in Frame 2, and continues the wave-like movement as he extends his leg back and down, until his leg is straight (Frame 3). Notice in Frame 3 that he finishes the kick with his foot below hip level but not excessively deep. In the final frame, Vladimir lifts his straightened leg for the recovery. Once his leg lifts above hip level on the recovery, he will re-bend for the next propulsive down-kick.

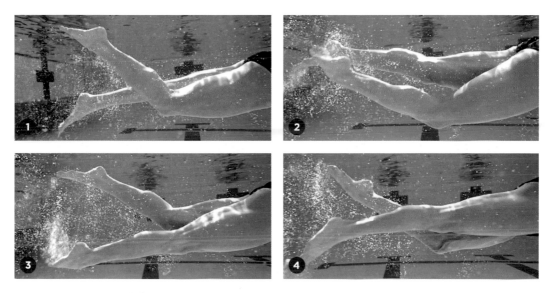

**FIGURE 3.3.** Vladimir Morozov kicking freestyle underwater.

Just as we saw propulsive similarities among strokes with the pull, so we see the same with the kick. Figure 3.4 on the next page shows Elizabeth kicking *back* and *down* for the propulsive phase of the butterfly kick. With bent knees, and feet facing back on the water, Elizabeth starts the kicking action by flexing her hips (Frame 1). She extends her lower legs, kicking back and down (Frame 2), and finishes the wave-like action with her legs fully extended and her feet below hip level (Frame 3).

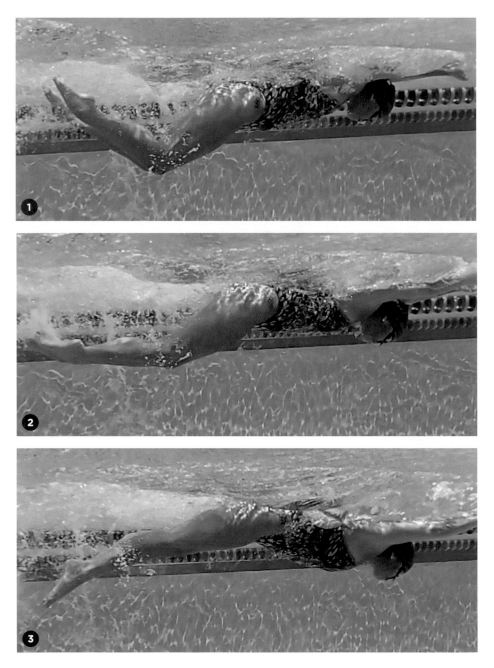

**FIGURE 3.4.** Elizabeth bends her knees so her feet face back on the water (1). She kicks back and down to full leg extension (2 and 3) for a powerful butterfly kick.

Figure 3.5 shows Aaron kicking in backstroke. Since Aaron is in a supine position, he kicks *back* and *up* rather than back and down, but the mechanics to do so are identical to those in freestyle and butterfly. Focusing on Aaron's left leg, you can see that he bends his knee to position the top of his foot facing back on the water (Frame 1), flexes his hip and kicks back and up (Frame 2), and ends the kick with his leg fully extended and straight (Frame 3).

**FIGURE 3.5.** Aaron feels lift and drag forces on the top of his left foot. He flexes his hip and kicks back and up for a propulsive backstroke kick.

## DO YOU MOVE BACKWARD WHEN YOU KICK?

Approximately 1 in 20 adults who attend my swim clinics ask how can it be possible that they move backward when they kick. These swimmers are bending their legs immediately when they finish the propulsive kick rather than recovering the leg straight until the foot reaches hip level and then bending. If a swimmer bends the knees too early, then the bottoms of the feet and backs of the lower legs will face forward in the water and apply force forward, which moves the swimmer backward. To fix the problem, these swimmers simply need to recover with a straight leg until the foot reaches hip level and then bend the leg in a last-moment preparation for the propulsive phase of the kick.

Breaststroke is in a class by itself when it comes to kicking. The breaststroke kick is the only kick that has a catch, operates in three dimensions, and connects with lift and drag on the bottom of the feet rather than the top. It gets special attention in the breaststroke chapter, but let's look now at how the feet face back on the water.

To position the feet facing back on the water, breaststrokers bend the knees just as swimmers do in the other strokes, but they must flex at the ankle and

**FIGURE 3.6.** NCAA champion and world championships medalist Laura Sogar faces her feet back on the water to utilize lift and drag forces to propel herself forward.

turn their feet out, rather than point and pigeon toe, to adhere to the rules of the stroke. Figure 3.6 shows Laura kicking in breaststroke. She bends her knees, flexes at the ankles, and turns her feet out. This positions the bottoms of her feet facing back on the water, as seen in both frames. Look closely at the photos and note the resistive pressure against the soles of Laura's feet. Lift and drag are making their presence known.

## CORE MOVEMENT AND FUNCTION

Let's switch gears and study the one component of the strokes that does not face back on the water—the core. It is impossible for the trunk of the body to position in such a way that it can press back against the water's resistance and overcome its own mass (the amount of "bad drag" it faces) to move a swimmer forward. The responsibility of propulsion falls solely on the limbs. However, while the core is not capable of generating propulsion, it is very much actively involved in the process of moving forward.

To actively involve the core in the process of moving forward, swimmers should think about core function in two ways. First, they must position the body to minimize bad drag. Bad drag cannot be avoided completely, but swimmers can control whether water flows past the body in a laminar (smooth) fashion or if it adheres to the body as it passes by. Swimmers align the head, torso, hips, and upper legs to feel the water flow past uninhibited. If the water seems to attach to a particular section of the body, such as the hips or upper legs, the swimmer can adjust pelvic tilt or body alignment to feel a more laminar, smooth flow.

The second core function is to move in rhythm with the momentum of the stroke. This involves moving the core on an axis of rotation rather than simply holding the aligned body mass static in the water. The strokes are divided into two categories based on the nature of the rotation. Butterfly and breaststroke are short-axis strokes, and freestyle and backstroke are long-axis strokes. The short axis is an imaginary line that runs from one side of the hips to the other side; the long axis is an imaginary line that runs the length of the body, from the top of the head through the belly button, dividing the right side of the body from the left side.

Swimmers in breaststroke and butterfly move their core on the short axis in an undulating action. The hips position near the surface of the water during all phases of the stroke as the body oscillates in rhythm on the short axis.

The photos in Figure 3.7 show Elizabeth driving forward on the short axis in butterfly. Notice that her hips remain at the surface as she undulates her core forward and down (Frame 1) and then forward and up (Frame 2). Her body is elastic and flexible yet never sags or loses tone in the water. Also, Elizabeth is always cognizant of how the water flows past her torso, hips, and upper legs, ensuring the flow is laminar at every moment in the stroke.

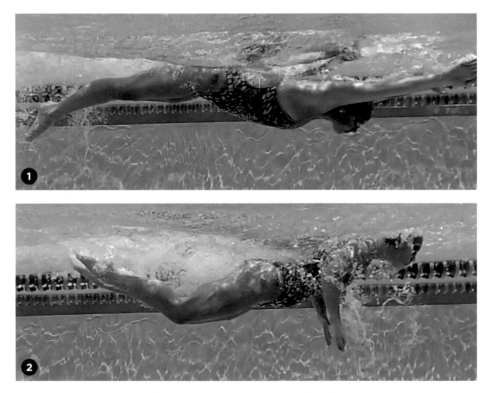

**FIGURE 3.7.** Elizabeth Beisel undulates on the short axis in butterfly.

Breaststrokers also keep the hips near the surface at all times as they move on the short axis. In Figure 3.8 Rebecca drives forward and up (Frame 1) and forward and down (Frame 2) on the short axis, never allowing her hips to drop or sag in the water. Rebecca does Pilates and yoga to strengthen her core, so she can control this short-axis movement.

**FIGURE 3.8.** Rebecca Soni drives her core along the short axis in breaststroke.

Freestylers and backstrokers position the core on a long axis of rotation. Whereas the challenge of short-axis strokes is to keep the hips at the surface at all times, the challenge during long-axis rotation is balancing the body side to side. The arms of backstrokers and freestylers move asynchronously, so the swimmer is not "squared off" as in butterfly and breaststroke. Swimmers who feel unbalanced during long-axis movement oftentimes use the limbs to compensate. They press their hand/arm to the side, or scissors-kick one leg to the side. This takes the hands, arms, and feet away from their primary purpose, which is to face back on the water and press against resistive forces to move forward.

The key to balancing on the long axis is to extend and catch properly. Swimmers must think about the chest, scapula, and arm extending *forward* on the side where the catch is taking place, and the hip rotating *up* on the other side of the body, where the hand/arm is finishing the stroke. Long-axis rotation is a diagonal movement (a slight twisting of the core), not a tipping of the skeletal frame on its side. One side extends; the other side rotates.

Figure 3.9 shows Peter extending forward on the long axis in freestyle. Note that his hip is up on the left side of his body, but his chest and arm extend forward on the right side as he makes the catch. By focusing on the catch, Peter establishes a stable platform and will not go off balance while his hips and lower core rotate with the momentum of the stroke on the long axis.

**FIGURE 3.9.** Peter Vanderkaay balances perfectly on the long axis as he makes his catch.

**FIGURE 3.10.** Aaron Peirsol extends for his catch as he rotates his hips on the long axis.

In Figure 3.10, Aaron drives his right hip up in backstroke as he extends his chest, scapula, and arm forward on the left side. Notice how his hips noticeably rotate between Frames 1 and 2, but his arm extends forward. Aaron concentrates on the catch with his left arm, providing a stable platform so he does not tip off balance while driving the hips and lower torso on the long axis.

## STROKE TIMING

We've covered several mechanical details relating to the pull, kick, and core movement. Don't let these overwhelm you. You are likely doing many things correctly already. There may be parts of the stroke you need to refine, or a few movements that need revamping, but that is what makes swimming interesting. Elite swimmers are refining their pull, kick, and core movement too.

They spend hours breaking down the strokes and training the individual components. They focus on the kick in isolation, or the pull, and they do core movement drills. Elite swimmers even train the components within a component; they will do drills during which they repeat the catch movement without progressing through the rest of the pull, or they will scull in a fixed position to strengthen the hands/forearms for a particular part of the stroke. This is how complex tasks are learned.

Eventually, though, every component must come together and work in time with the others if the most effective stroke is to emerge. The pull, kick, and core movement are like parts in a gear train system that turn on their own but connect with one another, like teeth in a cog. A swimmer can reach a certain maximum speed when pulling only, and a faster maximum speed when connecting a well-timed core movement with the pull, and yet an even faster maximum speed when adding a well-timed kick to the pull and core movement.

Studies conducted on the freestyle stroke in the 1980s revealed that the kick, when timed properly in the stroke, adds on average 10–12 percent to overall propulsion, and even went so high as to add a 27 percent increase in propulsion in some cases (Maglischo 2003, 38). Although research is lacking in the other three strokes, the general consensus among seasoned coaches is that the kick contributes at least as much to backstroke and butterfly propulsion. Since breaststroke is a two-cycle stroke—one pull and *then* one kick—the kick is credited for 50 percent of a breaststroker's propulsion.

The same study on freestyle propulsion, however, revealed that swimmers who do not time the kick properly with the pull and core movement, or who have poor kicking technique, can experience as much as a 6 percent *decrease* in propulsion when adding the kick to the arm stroke. Many readers can probably relate to this statistic. Triathletes are famous for not kicking because they fear it consumes energy without contributing to faster speeds. And triathletes are not the only ones. Go to any swim meet and you will see coaches on the deck shouting, "KICK!" They are willing their athletes to use their legs, but the swimmer in the water feels "off" when trying to do so. The athlete suspects the kick is not helping and feels that it wastes energy.

In each stroke, an effective kick steps in at very specific moments to support propulsion when the arms are either not propelling (during extension, for example) or are about to enter a stage of nonpropulsion. Even though swimmers appear to travel at a constant speed in the water, velocity studies show that forward movement changes throughout the stroke cycle. There are moments when the body decelerates and moments when the body accelerates, depending on the phase of the stroke cycle. Elite swimmers are masters at minimizing periods of deceleration due to impeccable timing. They carry momentum. They function the core properly and time the kick to show up when the pull is in need of support.

It is important that we study the timing so aspiring swimmers can take on elite timing and minimize periods of deceleration. But whereas we could compare the four strokes side by side when studying propulsion and core movement, timing and connection offer us little to compare. No stroke connects the cogs exactly like the others. Each is a unique dance. Butterflyers kick twice per arm pull and move on the short axis. Breaststrokers move on the short axis but kick only once per pull. Freestyle and backstroke are the closest we come to being able to make comparisons—both are long-axis strokes with 6 beats of the kick per arm pull (some freestylers kick with 2 or 4 beats, but 6 beats is most common), but the beats time differently with the pull and make these strokes two different dances.

The timing/connection of each stroke will be highlighted in the individual stroke chapters, but before leaving this chapter let's look at an inspiring moment in the stroke cycle that three of the four strokes share (breaststroke is the lone wolf once again due to its two-cycle nature). This example of timing showcases what it means to strategically time a kick within the stroke cycle.

During the finish of the stroke in butterfly, backstroke, and freestyle, elite swimmers combine the finish of the pull cycle with a propulsive kick to deliver what I call the Triple P—the power-packed punch. The Triple P occurs just before the swimmer recovers the arm(s) overwater. It is a boost in forward velocity at the finish of the stroke, before the deceleration that will occur while the swimmer recovers the arm(s) overwater and sets up for the catch on the next propulsive arm cycle. Studies reveal that elite swimmers' forward velocity peaks at the finish of the stroke in butterfly, backstroke, and freestyle, and this is due to the Triple P.

In Figure 3.11 Elizabeth times a propulsive kick with the finish of the arm cycle in butterfly. This is the Triple P. It gives Elizabeth a spike in forward velocity before the deceleration that will occur as she recovers her arms over the water. Elizabeth travels faster during this moment of the stroke than any other.

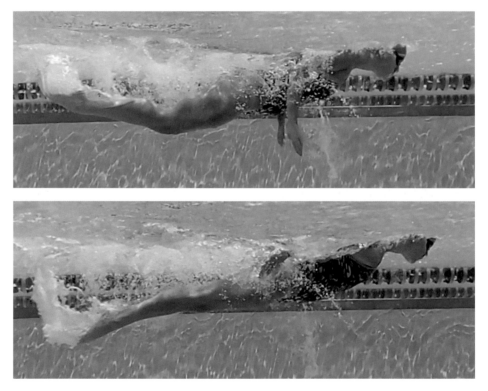

**FIGURE 3.11.** Elizabeth times a propulsive kick with the finish of the stroke to reach the fastest forward velocity she will attain during the entire stroke cycle.

In Figure 3.12 you can see that Aaron adds a power-packed punch to his backstroke finish by timing a propulsive up-kick with the final thrust of the arm stroke. The Triple P accelerates him forward.

**FIGURE 3.12.** Aaron connects a powerful kick with a strong finish to his pull in backstroke.

And what about the fastest man to ever take to water? In sprint mode, does Vladimir Morozov time and connect the pull and kick for the Triple P? You bet. Figure 3.13 on the next page shows Vladimir's power-packed punch.

**FIGURE 3.13.** Vladimir, the fastest man ever to take to water, connects the finish of his arm stroke with a propulsive down-kick—the Triple P.

# STROKE DATA

**BY NOW YOU'RE PROBABLY** ready to take a stroke or two out for a curvilinear test drive. Or maybe you're looking forward to connecting the pull, kick, and core movement of your favorite stroke for that power-packed punch we saw in the previous chapter. Regardless of what you work on, you'll be taking on Olympic-level techniques, which means you will not just swim faster, you will swim *effectively*.

Swimming effectively allows you to enjoy multiple gears in your swimming. You will be able to swim easy, moderate, fast, sprint, and in-between gears such as easy/moderate and moderate/fast. You will be in full control of the effort you put into your stroke (the gear you choose), and that effort will translate directly to the speed you travel. You will be able to choose the right gear for a race or the set you're doing in practice.

The key to swimming in various gears is to maintain your stroke mechanics no matter which speed you choose. Nelson Deibel, 1992 Olympic gold medalist in the 100-meter breaststroke, explains it succinctly: "You must hold the same amount of water when you want to go fast."

What does it mean to hold the same amount of water when you want to go fast? It means that rather than spinning your arms and kicking your legs in a flurry of activity when you want to go fast, you maintain your curvilinear path and continue to focus on the connection among the components, building power and speed within that connection. It means channeling your champion spirit in the right direction.

There is a valuable tool in swimming that lets you know if you are directing your energy the right way and holding water as you ratchet up the speed. It is called *stroke data.* Stroke data is a set of numbers that reveal the details behind the ultimate measure of success in swimming—*time.* Think of time like the final score of a baseball game, with stroke data the statistics behind the score.

In this chapter we will examine how stroke data is gathered and used. At the end of the chapter we will compare superstar swimmer and NBC Olympic commentator Rowdy Gaines's stroke technique and data today—as a masters world-record holder—to his technique and data from 33 years ago when he broke the world records in the 50-, 100-, and 200-meter freestyles. Through Rowdy's example, and through data charts presented at the end of each stroke-specific chapter, we will learn why stroke data is a valuable tool that all swimmers should understand and put to use.

## THE NUMBERS AND PROFICIENCY

Elite swimmers are not just great technicians. They take it a step further and are *proficient,* which means they effectively weave degrees of speed and power into their strokes. Stroke proficiency can be quantified using stroke data. Researchers and coaches have compiled stroke data on elite swimmers' performances for decades to study their proficiency. Any swimmer can gather stroke data on his or her own swims, and use elite swimmers' numbers as a model and a target, to make progress toward becoming as proficient as possible.

Building proficiency into your stroke requires understanding the relationship between two pieces of data:

- **Stroke count.** The number of stroke cycles you take to cover a distance.
- **Stroke rate.** The time it takes you to complete each stroke.

Stroke count and stroke rate are the details behind the time it takes you to cover a certain distance when you are on the surface stroking. Figure 4.2 illustrates. Let's say a swimmer pushes off the wall in a 25-meter pool and kicks in a streamline position underwater for 5 meters before breaking out to stroke (the breakout is the moment the swimmer surfaces after streamlining underwater). The distance the athlete swims at the surface is therefore 20 meters. Stroke count and stroke rate are taken during that 20 meters of swimming.

**FIGURE 4.1.** Vladimir Morozov streamlines underwater before breaking out to stroke.

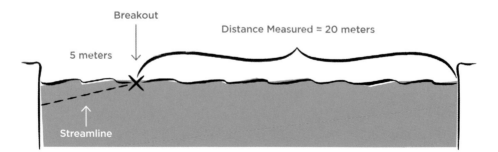

**FIGURE 4.2.** 25-meter pool.

## HOW TO TAKE YOUR STROKE COUNT

To take your stroke count, simply count each time your arms enter the water for a stroke. In breaststroke and butterfly this is a straightforward task since the arms move synchronously. In freestyle and backstroke you have two choices; you can count as each arm enters the water, or you can count in full stroke cycles, which is every time an arm on one side of the body enters the water—from right arm to right arm or left to left. It does not matter which way you count, but when comparing your count with others you need to use the same method.

In this book, stroke counts are gathered as *full stroke cycles*. If you prefer to count when each arm enters the water in freestyle and backstroke, that is fine. Simply divide your number in half to make the conversion to a full-stroke cycle count.

When you compare your stroke count with that of other swimmers, also note the size of the pool in which the data was taken. Competitions/practices are held in 25-yard, 25-meter, or 50-meter pools. Stroke counts obviously vary depending on the size of the pool.

Once the data is gathered, the numbers are entered into a simple mathematical equation that shows the details behind the swimmer's time for the 20 meters. The number of strokes the swimmer takes to cover a distance (stroke count), multiplied by the rate at which they take the strokes (stroke rate), equals the time (in seconds) to complete the distance. The equation looks like this:

(# strokes) x (rate) = time

Let's plug numbers in from our example. If a swimmer takes 10 full stroke cycles to cover the 20 meters, and if they complete each stroke in 2 seconds, then the swimmer's time for the 20 meters is 20 seconds, calculated like so:

(10 strokes) x (2 seconds per stroke) = 20 seconds

HOW TO TAKE YOUR STROKE RATE

**HOW TO TAKE YOUR STROKE RATE**

To take your stroke rate, have someone time how long it takes you to complete *one full stroke cycle.* Your timer will start the watch when your hand enters the water, and stop the watch when the hand enters again on the next cycle. The time it takes from entry to entry is your stroke rate. In breaststroke the hands are difficult to see, so I usually take rate each time the head lifts from the water. Rate should be taken multiple times during the swim to get an accurate number. Your timer should also note how long it takes for you to do 2 full stroke cycles and divide that number by 2 to minimize small errors in timing.

This equation shows swimmers that once they are on the surface stroking, there are only two ways to get faster. They can either take fewer strokes to cover the 20 meters or take their strokes at a faster rate. Simple enough, right? Lower one of the numbers and you will lower your time. Yes, in theory it is simple, but in real life it's more complicated. The two factors in our equation are not necessarily mutually exclusive. Oftentimes the efforts a swimmer makes to lower one number adversely affects the other number. Let's look at an example.

If data taken from an elite swimmer's performance in a 25-meter pool shows they covered 20 meters in 8 strokes (we will assume the swimmer streamline kicks underwater for 5 meters too), at a rate of 1.5 seconds per stroke, then the equation would look like this:

$$(8 \text{ strokes}) \times (1.5 \text{ seconds per stroke}) = 12 \text{ seconds}$$

The swimmer in our first example sees that the best athletes are 8 seconds faster than they are and that those athletes achieve that time by taking 2 fewer strokes at a slightly quicker rate. The elite swimmers' stroke count and rate numbers are not out of the realm of possibility for the aspiring swimmer. The numbers are exciting to chase. Our aspiring swimmer sets out to lower the stroke count from 10 to 8 by gliding the hand/arm out front before catching. The swimmer lowers the count to 8, which is thrilling, *but*... by passively gliding the hand/arm, the rate increases from 2.0 seconds per stroke cycle to 2.5 seconds per stroke cycle. The aspiring swimmer's equation now looks like this:

$$(8 \text{ strokes}) \times (2.5 \text{ seconds per stroke}) = 20 \text{ seconds}$$

The swimmer improved stroke count, but to the detriment of rate, and there is no improvement in time.

On the other side of the equation, if the swimmer sets out to quicken the rate without giving consideration as to how stroke count is affected, then they may end up in another stalemate. Swimmers who try to move their arms as quickly as possible to improve rate oftentimes find a path of lesser resistance by slipping the hand/arm through the water, or they take a shorter pull path by not making the catch overhead or by ignoring a directional change. The swimmer spins the arms quickly, but the flurry does not translate into moving the body forward as well as it could if mechanics were maintained. Stroke count increases, and the equation could look like this:

$$(12 \text{ strokes}) \times (1.7 \text{ seconds per stroke}) = 20.4 \text{ seconds}$$

The rate approaches the elite swimmer's rate, but stroke count drifts further away, and there is once again no improvement in time.

## SWIMMING EFFECTIVELY

Swimming effectively requires paying equal attention to both factors in the equation. Remember Nelson Deibel's statement? "Hold the same amount of water when you want to go fast."

"Going fast" refers to the *rate* side of the equation. Elite swimmers fire their muscles quickly when they want to go fast. But, they do so effectively by maintaining their mechanics to ensure the *stroke count* side of the equation. They always make the overhead catch, and they always navigate the directional changes to the diagonal and finish phases of the stroke. If the catch is rushed, or a directional change is skipped, then the propulsive path is shortened and the swimmer holds a lesser amount of water; efficacy declines.

As you work on your stroke count and stroke rate equation, regularly remind yourself to maintain your mechanics. Especially concentrate on making the catch overhead. Sear images in your mind like Figure 4.3 of Elizabeth Beisel making the catch in butterfly. Elizabeth is swimming at her 400-meter individual medley Olympic race-pace in this photo. She ensures the overhead catch, which helps her achieve an elite stroke count along with her race rate of turnover. The catch is the most difficult phase of the stroke to master at race speeds. Train it in slower gears, and build speed (rate) into it over time.

**FIGURE 4.3.** Elizabeth Beisel ensures a low stroke count by making a strong overhead catch even during race mode.

Elite swimmers also swim effectively by maintaining the connection between the pull, kick, and core movement, no matter which gear they choose. For example, elite backstrokers incorporate 6 beats of a kick per arm cycle whether stroking at an easy rate or an aggressive fast rate, and the beats occur at the same moment in the stroke cycle every time. When they go into high gears for fast swimming, the arms fire faster, the legs fire faster, and the core matches the momentum by driving on the axis faster. Everything speeds up, *not just the arms.*

Figure 4.4 shows Aaron Peirsol making the connection in backstroke. Whether he swims easy or fast, Aaron's core will always be in this position on

**FIGURE 4.4.** Aaron Peirsol always connects the pull with the kick and core movement, no matter which gear he's in.

the axis at this moment in the stroke—the catch—and the right leg will always be the propulsive leg (kicking up) at this moment in the stroke. Remind yourself to keep that connection when you want to pick up and go fast.

At the end of each stroke chapter you will find data charts showing stroke counts and rates taken from various elite performances, for both men and women. Study the numbers and gather data on your swims to make comparisons and determine where you can build proficiency in your stroke.

## THE UNDERWATER STREAMLINE KICK

To this point we have addressed only the time spent on the surface stroking. Now let's look at the part of the race that takes place underwater, while the swimmer kicks in a streamline position. In every stroke except for breaststroke, elite swimmers dolphin kick underwater before surfacing to stroke. (Note: Breaststrokers take what's called a breaststroke pullout, explained in the breaststroke chapter.)

The potential of the underwater kick was discovered when athletes with strong kicks learned they could travel the same distance taking two dolphin kicks underwater as they could taking one arm stroke cycle at the surface, *and*

**FIGURE 4.5.** U.S. national team member Melanie Margalis dolphin kicks in a streamline position underwater before surfacing to stroke.

that the rate to take the two kicks was quicker than the rate to take the one stroke cycle, making the underwater kick the better choice as a mode of travel.

As I mentioned in Chapter 2, swimmers pushed the limits holding their breath to take advantage of the newfound revelation, so the rulebooks were changed primarily for safety reasons, limiting athletes to 15 meters of underwater kicking. Just because swimmers are allowed to kick to the 15-meter mark, however, and just because kicking can be faster in some instances, does not mean that all elite athletes max out the 15 meters underwater. Not all swimmers' kicks are faster than their full strokes at the surface, and some athletes feel that the oxygen expenditure does not outweigh the gain in speed even if their kick is faster. Others do train to stay underwater and approach the 15-meter mark, having measured that they are faster by doing so and feel the loss of oxygen does not affect their race performance.

The data charts at the end of the stroke chapters provide information on the length of time elite swimmers stay underwater kicking, and at which meter mark they surface. You will see a range. Each swimmer is unique, and you are too. When deciding how long to kick underwater, note the elite swimmers' data, but make your decision based on what is most effective for you—and consider your oxygen needs. Also keep in mind that the distance traveled underwater does affect stroke count, so when you compare your count with those of Olympic swimmers, take into consideration this statistic. (Note: The technique for underwater dolphin kicking is highlighted in the butterfly and backstroke chapters.)

## THE TURN

In addition to stroke count, stroke rate, and time/distance spent underwater kicking, another key piece of information included in the data charts is the time spent making the turn. Too many swimmers lack sharp focus on their turns, which adds unnecessary seconds to their time. Elite swimmers use the turn to get ahead of the competition. Let's look at how they make the turn and how data is gathered on this part of the race.

Figure 4.6 shows Melanie Margalis turning in butterfly. The time that transpires during the change of direction—from when Melanie's hands touch the wall (Frame 1) to when her feet plant and push off the wall (Frame 5)—is critical. Mastering a fast turnaround requires that swimmers tuck the legs and feet, as we see Melanie does in Frames 2, 3, and 4. By tucking tightly, Melanie's feet take a straight path to the wall, and she is able to minimize bad drag on her legs. Elite swimmers even overlay their feet while drawing their legs toward the wall, as Melanie does in Frame 3. (Of course, by the time she plants her feet on the wall—Frame 5—she separates her feet for a solid push-off.)

The data charts in the stroke chapters include information on the amount of time that transpires from hand touch to feet plant in all strokes. Since freestylers and backstrokers do not touch the wall with their hand, the "hands to

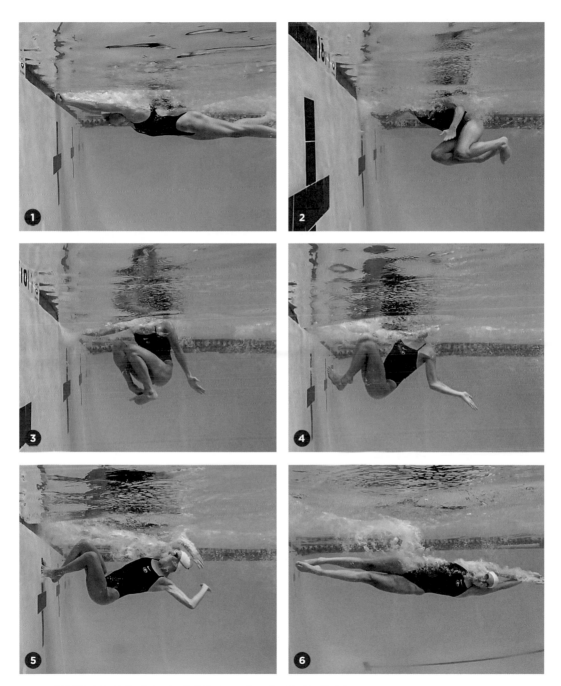

**FIGURE 4.6.** Melanie tucks tightly to make a fast butterfly turn.

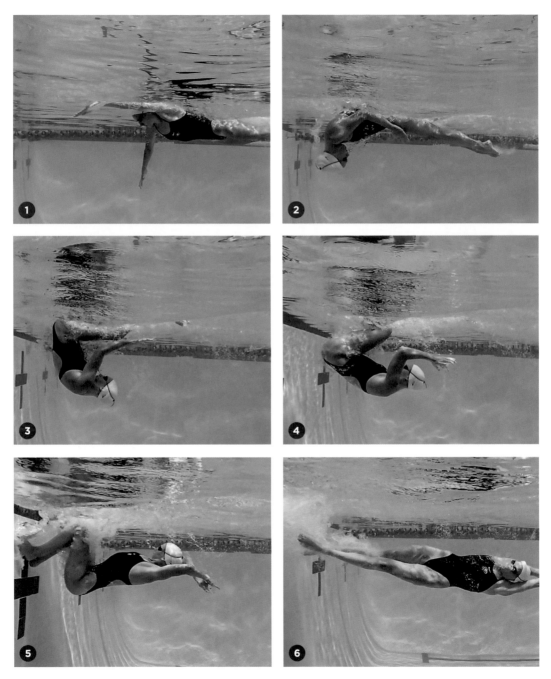

**FIGURE 4.7.** Melanie makes a change of direction quickly in the freestyle turn.

feet" time is calculated from when the hand enters the water on the last stroke before the turn, until the feet plant.

Figure 4.7 shows Melanie making a freestyle turn. The change of direction is timed from the moment her hand enters the water on her last stroke (Frame 1) until her feet plant on the wall (Frame 5). Melanie tucks tightly on the freestyle turn (Frames 3–5) just as she did during the butterfly turn. Notice also in Frames 3–5 that Melanie presses with her hands, which helps her speed up the rotation and get her legs to the wall quickly.

Let's sum up the data you will find in the charts at the end of each stroke chapter: The charts include stroke counts, stroke rates, the time and distance traveled underwater kicking, and the time it takes to make a turn. You will understand swimming from a unique angle by studying the numbers, and it will be a wonderful complement to your study of technique. Watch out, the numbers will draw you in!

## ROWDY GAINES—FREESTYLE STROKE DATA

I am thankful to coach Doc Counsilman for photographing the great Olympic swimmers of the 1960s, '70s, and '80s. I attended Doc's camp at Indiana University in 1981 as a 12-year-old, and one of the handouts was a black-and-white booklet filled with underwater stroke photos of Olympic champions and world-record holders, including Mark Spitz, Tracy Caulkins, Mary T. Meagher, Jim Montgomery, and Rowdy Gaines. Rowdy was the world-record holder in the 50-meter freestyle (22.96—long course, 1980), 100-meter freestyle (49.36—long course, 1981), and 200-meter freestyle (1:48.93—long course, 1982).

I studied the technique of the swimmers in the booklet for hours, even when I was 27 years old and still swimming with the hope of making my first Olympic team in 1996. This section on Rowdy Gaines has special meaning to me. The images Doc captured of Rowdy 33 years ago—that I studied relentlessly—are reprinted here alongside underwater photos of Rowdy's stroke today, as a world-record-setting masters swimmer in the 50–54 age group.

Alongside the photographs of Rowdy's stroke are data charts that highlight his stroke counts and rates, as well as time spent underwater and time to make the turn, from two 200-meter freestyle performances—one from 1980 and one from 2011.

The charts, combined with the photographs, bring home the concepts in this book. We see how the length of the curvilinear path affects our (# strokes) × (rate) equation, and what it means to change gears. Most important, through Rowdy's data we discern the details that underlie elite performance. They are definable, measureable numbers that all swimmers can target.

Thanks to the International Swimming Hall of Fame, I was able to track down video from the 1980 U.S. Olympic Swimming Trials. The United States boycotted the 1980 Olympic Games, which were hosted by the Soviet Union, but the U.S. swimming trials were held nonetheless. Rowdy won the 200-meter freestyle in 1:50.02. Following is his stroke data from that swim.

## Rowdy's Stroke Data—1980 U.S. Olympic Trials

**200-meter freestyle, 50-meter pool**
**Time: 1:50.02 (U.S. Olympic trials champion)**

| METERS | # OF STROKES* | RATE (S/STROKE CYCLE) | SPLIT |
|---|---|---|---|
| 1st 50 | 18 | 1.25 | 26.0 |
| 2nd 50 | 20 | 1.25 | 53.7 (27.7) |
| 3rd 50 | 20.5 | 1.25 | Not available |
| 4th 50 | 22.5 | 1.15 | 1:50.02 |

*Stroke counts listed as full stroke cycles*

**START AND TURN DATA**
Time and distance underwater off start: 2.6 s, 7 m
Time and distance underwater off turns: 1.7 s, 4–5 m
Hand-to-feet time on turns: 1.0–1.2 s

In 2011, at age 52, Rowdy competed in the 200-meter freestyle at a masters swim meet in Japan. His time was 2:03.51. Following is the data from that swim.

## Rowdy's Stroke Data—2011

**2011 masters swim meet in Japan, 50–54 age group**
**200-meter freestyle, 50-meter pool**
**Time: 2:03.51 (1st place)**

| METERS | # OF STROKES· | RATE (S/STROKE CYCLE) | SPLIT |
|---|---|---|---|
| 1st 50 | 18.5 | 1.35–40 | 27.05 |
| 2nd 50 | 20 | 1.40 | 58.44 (31.39) |
| 3rd 50 | 20.5 | 1.40–1.43 | Not available |
| 4th 50 | 21 | 1.45 | 2:03.51 |

*Stroke counts listed as full stroke cycles*

**START AND TURN DATA**
Time and distance underwater off start: 2.6 s, 7 m
Time and distance underwater off turns: 1.7 s, 4–5 m
Hand-to-feet time on turns: 1.0–1.2 s

## COMPARING DATA BETWEEN THE TWO SWIMS

The numbers are revealing. First, note that Rowdy's stroke count was nearly identical over the course of both 200s. Overall, he took 1 stroke less for the 200 meters as a 52-year-old than he did as a 21-year-old (80 strokes in 2011, and 81 strokes in 1980). If we look at Rowdy's stroke technique in 1981 compared with his technique today (Figures 4.8 and 4.9 on the next page), we see that his pull path has not changed. He "holds the same amount of water." Rowdy makes the overhead catch and navigates the same directional changes to the diagonal and finish phases of the stroke today that he did 33 years ago. Because his curvilinear path is the same, his stroke length is the same, and this makes his stroke count the same.

**FIGURE 4.8.** Rowdy Gaines's freestyle stroke, 1981.

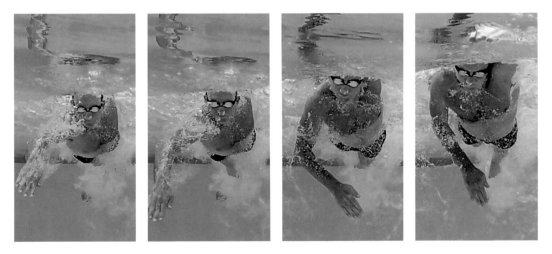

**FIGURE 4.9.** Rowdy's freestyle stroke, 2013.

So what accounts for the difference in time, from a 1:50.02 in 1980 to the 2:03.51 in 2011? Rowdy's time and distance underwater after the start and turns are the same. We see from the data compilation that it is the *rate* that accounts for the 13-second time difference. At first glance it does not appear that his 1.25 rate from 1980 is so much different from his 1.35–1.40 stroke rate from the 2011 race. It's only about one-tenth of a second different. But look at how it adds up over the course of 50 meters, and even more so over the course of 200.

Let's use data from the second 50 as our first example, because Rowdy's stroke count was identical on that 50 from 1980 and 2011. If we enter his data into our (# strokes) × (rate) swimming equation, here is what we get:

From his second 50 in 1980:

**(20 strokes) x (1.25 seconds per stroke) = 25 seconds\***

On the second 50 in 2011, Rowdy took 20 strokes at a rate of 1.40 seconds per stroke:

**(20 strokes) x (1.40 seconds per stroke) = 28 seconds**

We see that this ever-so-slightly slower rate adds up over the course of 20 stroke cycles on the second 50. There is a difference of 3 seconds from 1980 to 2011 on the stroking portion of that 50. Simple math tells us that 3 seconds difference per 50 adds up to 12 seconds for the 200. (Note: Rowdy's rate went up slightly more on the last two 50s in 2011, accounting for the additional 1.5 seconds.)

I am not saying that Rowdy should get to work and bring back the 1.25 rate of his youth. Training does impact an athlete's ability to go into faster gears while holding the same amount of water. Rowdy trains much less today than he did in the 1980s, and age impacts rate as well. The ability to fire the muscles at fast speeds surely declines to some degree over time, but by incorporating a few fast-firing swim sets into training, masters swimmers can approach some pretty fast gears.

---

\* Keep in mind that 25 seconds is not the full time for Rowdy's second 50. We have to add in the time underwater off the first turn (1.7 seconds) as well as the time spent making the turn at the 100 (approximately 1.0 second). These two pieces of data add 2.7 seconds to the 25 seconds, to give us a total of 27.7 for the second 50.

Also, it must be noted that a 1.25 rate is not the prescribed rate for all athletes. Most elite male middle-distance freestylers stroke in the range of 1.35–1.60 per stroke cycle for 200 meters. Athletes who stroke in this 1.35–1.60 range have a longer propulsive pull path and take fewer strokes. For instance, during Rowdy's era one of the most famous male middle-distance swimmers was Michael Gross, from Germany. Gross is 6 feet 7 inches tall and nicknamed "the Albatross" for his giant arm span of nearly 7 feet. On his second 50 of the 200-meter freestyle on the 4 × 200-meter freestyle relay at the 1984 Olympics, Gross took 16 strokes at a rate of 1.6 seconds per stroke. His equation looked like this:

$$\text{(16 strokes)} \times \text{(1.6 seconds per stroke)} = 25.6 \text{ seconds}$$

Stroke length is individual, as is stroke rate. There is a range, however. In this book, you will see that proficiency is achieved through varying combinations of stroke count and rate, but you will also note that if one factor drifts toward the outer edges of the range, the other factor must balance the equation.

Study the numbers and have fun chasing them. Understanding the data made a world of difference in my training and racing, and I think it will in yours too.

Thanks, Rowdy! Let's plan another photo shoot for 2034!

## CHASE ROWDY

If you train in a 25-yard pool and want to compare your numbers to Rowdy's, here is data taken from a 100-yard freestyle swim Rowdy did at the 2010 U.S. Masters Swimming Championships at age 51.

## Rowdy's Short-Course Yards Data

2010 U.S. Masters Swimming Championships, 50–54 age group
100-yard freestyle, 25-yard pool
Time: 46.90 (1st place)

| YARDS | # OF STROKES* | RATE (S/STROKE CYCLE) | SPLIT |
|-------|---------------|------------------------|-------|
| 1st 25 | 6 | 1.20 | Not available |
| 2nd 25 | 8 | 1.25 | 22.34 |
| 3rd 25 | 7.5 | 1.25 | Not available |
| 4th 25 | 8.5 | 1.25 | 46.90 (24.56) |

*Stroke counts listed as full stroke cycles

### START AND TURN DATA

Time and distance underwater off start: 2.9 s, 8–9 yards
Time and distance underwater off turns: 1.8–2.0 s, approximately 5 yards
Hand-to-feet time on turns: 1.0–1.2 s

# 5

## BUTTERFLY

**WHEREAS FREESTYLE HAS BEEN** on the Olympic swimming schedule since 1896, backstroke since 1900, and breaststroke since 1904, butterfly did not make its Olympic debut until more than a half century later, in 1956. Swimming organizers were not simply seeking to add another stroke to the sport's lineup; rather, butterfly was created as a stroke to preserve the purity of breaststroke. Prior to the 1950s the rules governing swimming stated that during the breaststroke arm action, "both hands must be moved forward together and brought backwards simultaneously" (*FINA Handbook* 1937). Nothing stipulated whether the hands had to be recovered *under* versus *over* the water, so swimmers in the 1930s improved upon what had been the conventional breaststroke technique—in which the arms were recovered under the water—and lifted their arms over the water in a manner we know today as the butterfly recovery. The result was a perfectly legal variant of breaststroke that was dubbed the "butterfly-breaststroke"—a combination of the butterfly arm stroke with the breaststroke kick.

The 1936 Olympic 200-meter breaststroke final (men) featured a race in which some swimmers employed the conventional breaststroke technique while others switched back and forth between the butterfly-breaststroke technique and the conventional breaststroke. By 1952 the butterfly-breaststroke had taken over and was favored by nearly all athletes. Gold medals in Helsinki 1952 were won by butterfly-breaststrokers in both the men's and women's breaststroke events. This was bothersome to many swimming purists, so to preserve the breaststroke technique as it was originally intended, FINA (Federation Internationale de Natation Amateur—the International Swimming Federation) created a new stroke, called the "butterfly," in 1953.

The 1953–1956 *FINA Handbook* clarified that in breaststroke the hands must be "brought forward together from the breast *on or under* the surface of the water," and in butterfly the arms must be "brought forward together *over* the water." Guidelines for the butterfly kick were established in the handbook as well. The 1956 Olympic Games, held in Melbourne, Australia, were the first to feature the butterfly stroke. The 200-meter butterfly was added for men (William Yorzyk of the United States won gold in 2:19.3), and the 100-meter butterfly for women (Shelley Mann of the United States won gold in 1:11.0). The 4 × 100 medley relay was added to the Olympic schedule four years later.

In this chapter we are fortunate to have elite butterflyers Elizabeth Beisel, Ariana Kukors, and Doug Reynolds showcase the pull, kick, and core movement of this fantastic, and relatively young, Olympic stroke.

## THE PULL PATTERN

To begin our review of butterfly technique, let's look at the curvilinear pull pattern from start to finish. Figure 5.1 shows Elizabeth swimming butterfly from hand entry in Frame 1 to the finish of the stroke in Frame 8.

In Frame 1 Elizabeth enters and extends her arms overhead, directly in front of her shoulders. It is important to enter and extend in line with the shoulders to minimize head-on resistance during this nonpropulsive phase of the arm cycle. In Frames 2–4 the propulsive arm action becomes the focus—as

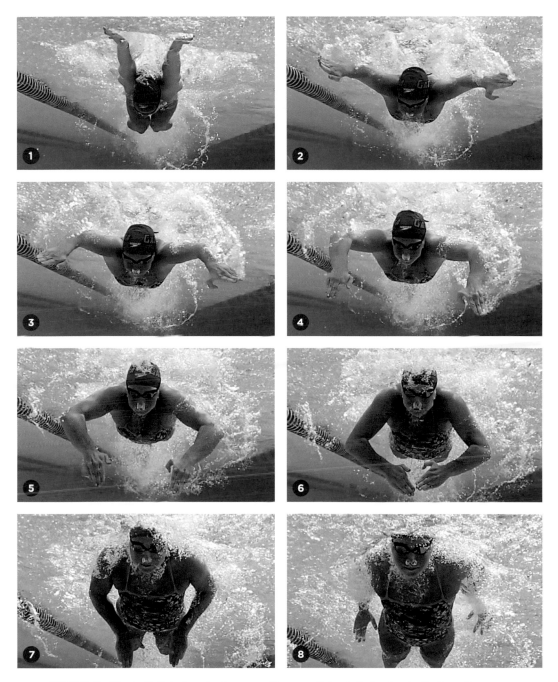

**FIGURE 5.1.** Elizabeth Beisel navigates a curvilinear path back during her butterfly pull.

Elizabeth sweeps outside shoulder width to make a strong catch. She connects with lift and drag forces by positioning her hands/forearms facing back on the water, and locks onto that connection throughout the diagonal phase of the stroke (Frames 5 and 6) and the finish (Frames 7 and 8).

The back-facing position of the hands/forearms throughout the pull cycle is critical for forward-directing propulsion. It starts with the catch. Figure 5.2 shows how Doug positions his hands/forearms to face back on the water as he makes the catch.

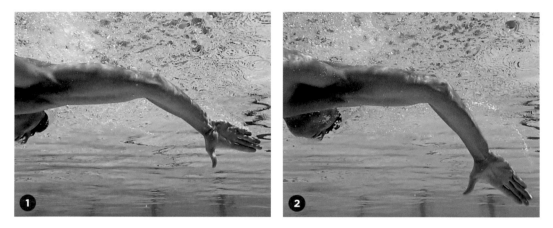

**FIGURE 5.2.** Doug Reynolds positions his hand/forearm to face back on the water as he makes the catch in Frame 2.

Swimmers must ensure that the hands/forearms face back on the water even during directional changes. Figure 5.3 of Ariana shows that her hands/arms face back on the water as she maneuvers the limbs under her body during the diagonal phase of the stroke. Notice also Ariana's hand/arm tone, finger spacing, and that her wrists are straight—hands held in line with forearms—to form one giant stroking paddle. This single photo captures the essence of elite-level stroking. Ariana holds her limbs in such a way as to feel the water's resistive forces, and she positions her limbs so those forces can be used to propel herself *forward*. With both arms holding the water at the same time in butterfly, the pull is a powerful source of propulsion.

**FIGURE 5.3.** Ariana presses back on the water during the diagonal phase of the stroke, using her hands and forearms as giant paddles.

> ### HAND ACCELERATION
>
> As discussed in Chapter 2, developing an elite-level feel for the water requires that you increase your hand speed (and hence your hand force) as you progress through the pull cycle. Hand speed is slowest during the catch and fastest at the finish of the stroke. Elite swimmers accelerate water back at the finish of the stroke.

## STROKE TIMING AND CORE MOVEMENT

Swimming rules do not mandate a set number of dolphin kicks per arm pull, but elite swimmers kick twice per stroke cycle to maximize forward velocity. They kick at strategic points in the stroke cycle—when the hands enter the water and extend, and again when the hands finish the stroke and exit the water. The legs must be recovered up between kicks. Let's look at the timing of these actions, as well as the complementary core movement.

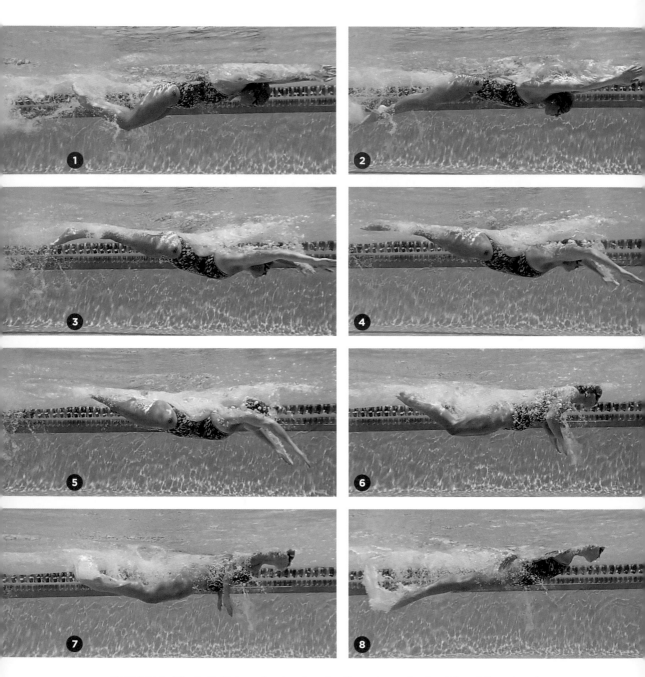

**FIGURE 5.4.** Elizabeth kicks as her hands enter the water and extend (1 and 2) and again as her hands finish the pull and exit the water (7 and 8).

Figure 5.4 shows Elizabeth swimming butterfly from entry to the finish. In Frame 1 her hands/arms enter the water, and she simultaneously begins the first kick. She completes the kicking action as she extends her arms overhead (Frame 2). The kick is vital at this moment—it helps Elizabeth maintain forward velocity since her arms are not propulsive during this part of the stroke cycle. Notice also that during the first kick, Elizabeth presses her head and chest *down* and *forward,* which results in a slightly pike body position—with hips at the peak (Frame 2). By moving the core on the axis in this manner, water flows smoothly past the body and upper legs, minimizing resistance, and thus minimizing deceleration.

After finishing the first kick, Elizabeth recovers her legs up *in a straight-leg position* and attends to the details of the catch, as seen in Frames 3–5. To keep the body moving forward on the axis, Elizabeth straightens her body and lifts her head slightly during the catch (see sidebar on page 94).

As Elizabeth progresses through the diagonal phase of the pull, she bends her legs to set up for the second kick (Frame 6). Timing the kick properly during these moments (specifically timing the knee bend) puts Elizabeth in a great position for the power-packed punch—the combination of the finish of the arm stroke with a propulsive second kick (Frames 7 and 8).

The spike in forward velocity during the Triple P, coupled with a toned, straight core, as we see in Frame 8, ensures that Elizabeth will not decelerate drastically as her arms enter the non-propulsive overwater recovery phase of the stroke (and as the legs recover up to prepare for the first kick in the next stroke cycle).

To help recover your arms overwater in butterfly, snap your legs up quickly after the Triple P (*straight-leg recovery at first,* then bend the knees before the arms enter the water). Do not allow the legs to sit low in the water after the propulsive Triple P down-kick. A quick leg recovery helps you drive your hips forward and aids your arm recovery forward.

## HEAD MOVEMENT

Movement of the head during the stroke cycle is slight but important. Figure 5.4 shows the position of Elizabeth's head as she progresses through the phases of the pull. In Frames 1 and 2 Elizabeth's head rides just below the water surface, and she directs her gaze down, while entering her arms in the water and extending forward. Her core undulates down and forward on the short axis, following the head just under the surface of the water, during these moments in the stroke cycle. In Frames 3–5 she raises her head and her gaze slightly as she makes the catch. This starts the core moving up and forward on the axis. In butterfly, the head leads the core's undulation motion throughout the stroke—down and forward during entry and extension, and up and forward during the catch, diagonal, and finish phases of the stroke. If the head directs forward, the body will direct forward. Never dive the head too deeply or lift it too high. Undulate forward just as Elizabeth does.

Figure 5.5 shows the head movement from a front view. Elizabeth directs her gaze down, and presses her chest down and forward, during entry and extension (Frame 1). She lifts her head and gaze slightly, to lead the core forward, as she makes the catch (Frame 2).

**FIGURE 5.5.** Elizabeth directs her gaze down during entry and extension (1). She lifts her head slightly during the catch to lead the core forward (2).

**FIGURE 5.6.** Ariana uses core strength to keep her hips at the surface as she finishes and recovers her arms overwater.

Figure 5.6 shows Ariana finishing the stroke with the Triple P in Frame 1 and holding her body in line near the water's surface as she recovers the arms overwater. Even as she begins to bend her knees (Frame 2) for the upcoming first kick of the next stroke cycle, notice that she keeps her hips at the surface rather than allowing them to sink. This takes great lower core strength, since the weight of the arms over the water naturally pushes down on the hips. Keep your hips near the surface during all phases of the butterfly stroke, especially during this most challenging finish and recovery phase.

Let's look at Ariana's finish and recovery from an above-water perspective. Figure 5.7 shows that she recovers with straight arms over the water. Elite butterflyers recover with straight arms; however, it is important to note that *the arms do not straighten until the hands exit the water after the finish phase of the pull.* Keep a bend in the elbow while finishing the pull, so the hands/ forearms face back on the water rather than push up on the water. In Frame 1, notice that Ariana's arms are bent and face back on the water as she finishes the propulsive stroke cycle. The upper arms and elbows leave the water first, followed by the forearms and hands. Once her hands exit the water, only then does Ariana fully extend her elbows for a straight-arm overwater recovery, as seen in the last three frames.

You can also see that Ariana's head, back, and shoulders ride just above the surface of the water. She drives forward without excessive up-and-down motion. When undulating on the short axis in butterfly, think *forward*, not up and down.

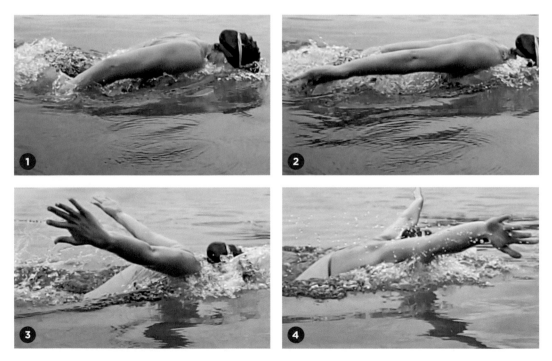

**FIGURE 5.7.** Ariana keeps her elbows bent as she finishes the underwater pull (1), and then extends for a straight-arm overwater recovery (2-4).

## THE BREATH

So that the lifting action does not inhibit forward momentum, it's important to breathe at the correct moment in the stroke cycle. Butterflyers lift their head and shoulders from the water during the back half of the pull—the diagonal and finish phases.

Figure 5.8 shows Ariana taking a breath. Notice that her head remains in the water as she makes the catch (Frame 1). As she navigates to the diagonal phase, she begins to lift her head and shoulders (Frame 2). By the time her hands/arms transition to the finish and overwater recovery phases of the stroke, as seen in Frames 3 and 4, she has cleared the water for the breath. Notice that Ariana does not lift her head and shoulders straight up in abrupt fashion. She lifts gradually and keeps her chin near the water's surface. Elite butterflyers channel their energy forward when breathing, to maintain forward velocity.

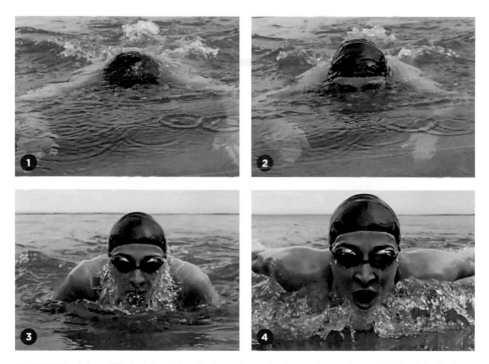

**FIGURE 5.8.** Ariana lifts her head for the breath gradually as she navigates the back half of the butterfly pull.

Return the face/head back to the water before the arms recover to the front of the stroke. Figure 5.9 shows Ariana taking a breath while her arms are behind her, and then lowering her head in the water before her arms recover forward for the next stroke cycle. Remember that the head leads the core forward on the axis, including when taking a breath, so proper breathing technique and timing are crucial for your best swimming.

**FIGURE 5.9.** After taking a breath, Ariana returns her head to the water before her arms recover to the front of the stroke.

## THE UNDERWATER DOLPHIN KICK

Whether your race strategy involves taking just 2–3 quick dolphin kicks off the walls or kicking the full 15 meters allowed underwater, you should get the most power from every kick. To do so requires that you incorporate the same undulation action with your core during your streamline kick that you use during the full stroke.

Figure 5.10 shows Doug dolphin kicking underwater. Notice how he undulates his body during the kicking action. He does not keep his body flat, kicking from the knees only. He presses his core down and forward (Frames 2–4) as he extends his legs for the down-kick. Although Doug uses his body to

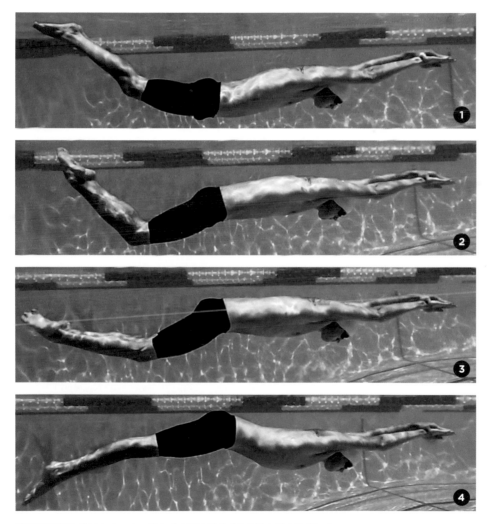

**FIGURE 5.10.** Doug powers the dolphin kick from the chest down.

kick underwater, take note in every frame that his arms direct straight ahead. He does not dive the arms up and down as he undulates the core. Keep the arms pointing straight ahead as you power the kick from the chest down.

## PRACTICE DRILL

Ariana's favorite drill for training a powerful, fast kick is "vertical dolphin kicking." Figure 5.12 on the next page shows Ariana demonstrating the drill. In Frame 1 she has just finished kicking forward and is recovering with straight legs back. In Frames 2 and 3 she bends her knees to set up for the next kick. In Frame 4 she flexes her powerful hips to begin the kicking action and continues with a wave-like movement through to the tips of her toes as she extends her legs in Frames 5 and 6. Ariana, like Doug, uses her entire body in the kicking action, not just her legs.

Figure 5.11 shows that Ariana has two degrees of difficulty for this drill. In version 1 she kicks with arms bent and hands/forearms out of the water (Frame 1). In version 2—the more difficult version—Ariana kicks with her arms held overhead in a streamline position (Frame 2).

**FIGURE 5.11.** Ariana has two degrees of difficulty for vertical dolphin kicking—forearms/hands out of water (1), and the more challenging streamline position (2).

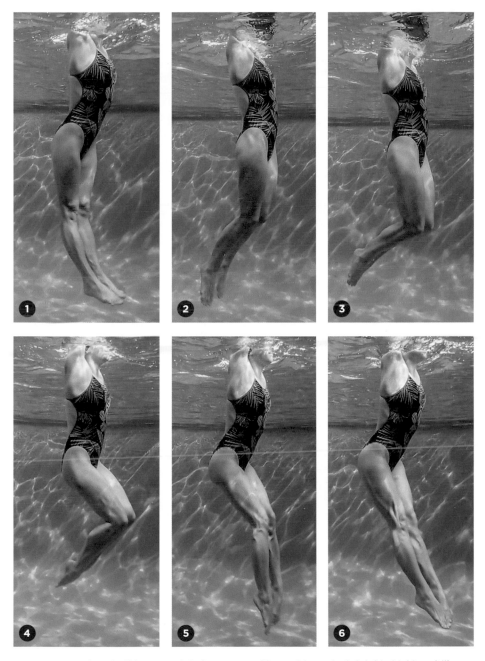

**FIGURE 5.12.** Ariana builds strength in her core and legs with vertical dolphin kicking drills.

You will get world-record strong if you can kick 4–8 sets in these positions for 20 seconds or more each set!

———

To feel the rhythm and beauty of this youngest Olympic stroke—butterfly—develop strength in your upper body, legs, and core. Most important, though, study and practice the curvilinear pull path, and timing of the kick, and core movement in this chapter, and you will soon be flying down the pool!

## STROKE DATA

### Dana Vollmer, 2012 Olympics—London

**100-meter butterfly, 50-meter pool**
**Time: 55.98 (gold medal and world record)**

| METERS | # OF STROKES | RATE (S/STROKE CYCLE) | SPLIT |
|--------|--------------|------------------------|-------|
| 1st 50 | 21 | 1.05–1.10 | 26.39 |
| 2nd 50 | 23 | 1.05–1.10 | 55.98 (29.59) |

**START AND TURN DATA**
Time and distance underwater off start: 4.4 s, 11 m
Time and distance underwater off turns: 3.3 s, 7–8 m
Hand-to-feet time on turns: 0.90 s

## Michael Phelps, 2012 Olympics—London

**100-meter butterfly, 50-meter pool**
**Time: 51.21 (gold medal)**

| METERS | # OF STROKES | RATE (S/STROKE CYCLE) | SPLIT |
|---|---|---|---|
| 1st 50 | 17 | 1.15 | 24.35 |
| 2nd 50 | 18 | 1.15 | 51.21 (26.86) |

### START AND TURN DATA
Time and distance underwater off start: 5.2 s, 13–14 m
Time and distance underwater off turns: 4.7 s, 11 m
Hand-to-feet time on turns: 0.95 s

## Elizabeth Beisel, 2014 NCAA Division I Swimming Championships

**400-yard individual medley, 25-yard pool**
**Time: 3:58.84**
**Butterfly split: 55.95**

| YARDS | # OF STROKES | RATE (S/STROKE CYCLE) | SPLIT |
|---|---|---|---|
| 1st 25 | 5 | 1.15 | Not available |
| 2nd 25 | 8 | 1.25 | 26.17 |
| 3rd 25 | 8 | 1.25–1.30 | Not available |
| 4th 25 | 8 | 1.25–1.30 | 55.95 (29.78 for 2nd 50 yards of 100) |

### START AND TURN DATA
Time and distance underwater off start: 6.0 s, 14 yards
Time and distance underwater off turns: 3.4 s, 8 yards
Hand-to-feet time on turns: 0.95–1.0 s

## Doug Reynolds, 2014 NCAA Division I Men's Swimming Championships

**100-yard butterfly, 25-yard pool**
**Time: 45.92**

| YARDS | # OF STROKES | RATE (S/STROKE CYCLE) | SPLIT |
|---|---|---|---|
| 1st 25 | 5 | 0.95–1.0 | 9.81 |
| 2nd 25 | 5 | 1.0 | 21.63 (11.82) |
| 3rd 25 | 5 | 1.0 | 33.53 (11.90) |
| 4th 25 | Not available | 1.05 | 45.92 (12.39) |

**START AND TURN DATA**
Time and distance underwater off start: 5.0 s, 15 yards
Time and distance underwater off turns: 6.2 s, 15 yards
Hand-to-feet time on turns: 1.0 s

*Note: Due to television coverage, data on some lengths not available.*

## Ariana Kukors, 2009 World Championships—Rome, Italy

**200-meter individual medley, 50-meter pool**
**Time: 2:06.15 (gold medal and world record)**
**Butterfly split: 27.72**

| METERS | # OF STROKES | RATE (S/STROKE CYCLE) | SPLIT |
|---|---|---|---|
| 1st 50 | 22 | 1.03 | 27.72 |

**START DATA**
Time and distance underwater off start: 5.0 s, 12 m

**SHEILA T. CLASSIC PICK**
# Mary T. Meagher ("Madame Butterfly")

1981 U.S. National Championships
200-meter butterfly, 50-meter pool
Time: 2:05.96 (gold medal and world record)

| METERS | # OF STROKES | RATE (S/STROKE CYCLE) | SPLIT |
|---|---|---|---|
| 1st 50 | 23 | 1.15 | 29.53 |
| 2nd 50 | 25 | 1.15–1.20 | 1:01.41 (31.88) |
| 3rd 50 | 26 | 1.15–1.20 | 1:33.69 (32.28) |
| 4th 50 | 26 | 1.10–1.15 | 2:05.96 (32.27) |

### START AND TURN DATA

Time and distance underwater off start: 3.1 s, 8 m
Time and distance underwater off turns: 1.8 s, 5 m
Hand-to-feet time on turns: 1.0 s

BACKSTROKE

# BACKSTROKE

**TO LAUNCH OUR DISCUSSION** of backstroke technique, let's consider a statement from Eddie Reese, head coach of the eight-time NCAA champion University of Texas men's swim team, and head U.S. Olympic swim coach in 2004 and 2008. When asked to write about his approach to butterfly and backstroke training, he is emphatic about the crucial and close correlation between stroke mechanics and speed:

> *The key to optimum speed in fly or back is to make the strokes as mechanically solid as possible. For example, there are many nationally ranked 11–12-year-olds in the backstroke who put their hand in the water on its back instead of perpendicular to the water. In the finals of U.S. Nationals or NCAAs, there may be one swimmer every four or five years whose hand entry is incorrect. At the highest levels of competition, fewer stroke technique errors are observed because the fastest swimmers are those with the most efficient technique. (Reese 2001, 271)*

Practicing and polishing proper mechanics in backstroke is particularly challenging because at no point during the stroke cycle can the swimmer see the position of their limbs to ensure correct technique. In every other stroke, swimmers can see their hands and arms in action, at least during the trickiest phase of the stroke—the catch. Since this is not possible with backstroke, swimmers must be meticulous in their attention to detail, and they must raise their proprioceptive abilities to the highest levels when practicing backstroke.

In this chapter we have the opportunity to study the mechanics of two of the best backstrokers in the world—Elizabeth Beisel and Aaron Peirsol. Their technique and stroke timing provide the guide we need. It is our task, then, to take what we learn from that technique and build those mechanics into our own backstroke.

## THE PULL PATTERN

Let's kick off our study by looking at the full length of the curvilinear pull pattern so we can see how the hand/arm positions throughout the propulsive stroke cycle. Figure 6.1 shows Aaron navigating the pull path from hand entry to finish.

In Frame 1 Aaron's left arm enters the water completely straight, in line with his shoulder, with palm facing out (hand perpendicular to the water). In Frames 2 and 3 he attends to the catch details, positioning his hand/forearm facing back on the water. Aaron cannot see that his hand and forearm face back on the water, but through hours of practice he has honed the skill of precise positioning. One of Aaron's favorites drills, detailed later in this chapter, involves isolating the catch moment of the stroke and repeatedly positioning the limb to face back on the water after the straight-arm entry.

Note the depth of Aaron's catch in Frame 3. His hand/arm is deep enough to allow him to sweep *up* during the diagonal phase of the stroke (Frames 4 and 5) and still keep his hand in the water—but no deeper. If he catches too deep he will be in a mechanically weak position with too much torque on his shoulder.

**FIGURE 6.1.** Aaron Peirsol navigates the curvilinear pull path in backstroke.

Aaron navigates the diagonal phase of the stroke in Frames 4 and 5 and the finish phase in Frames 6–8. Throughout the underwater pull, he makes sure that the resultant force of lift and drag directs back on the water, propelling him forward.

The rear-angle perspective shown in Figure 6.2 offers an even clearer view of the hand/forearm positioning, pressing back on the water at every phase of the stroke. Aaron catches in Frame 2, makes his first directional change to the diagonal phase in Frame 3, and makes his second directional change to the finish phase in Frame 4.

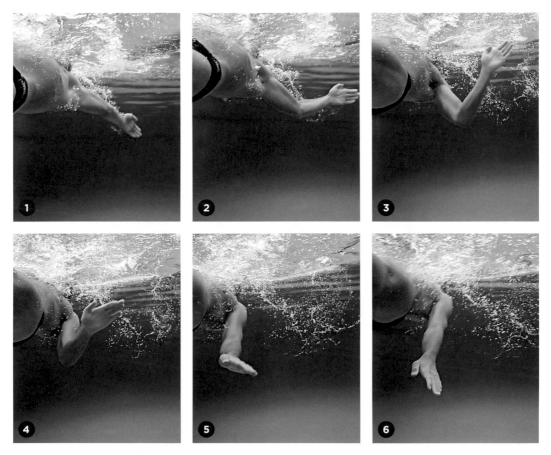

**FIGURE 6.2.** Aaron navigates the catch, diagonal, and finish phases of the backstroke pull.

## HAND ACCELERATION

Remember from Chapter 2 that developing an elite-level feel for the water requires that you increase your hand speed (and hence your hand force) as you progress through the backstroke pull cycle. Hand speed is slowest during the catch and fastest at the finish of the stroke. Elite swimmers accelerate water back at the finish of the stroke.

Backstrokers end the propulsive pull with a straight arm and with their hand below hip level, as seen in Frames 5 and 6. Since they are in a supine position, this is the best option for lengthening the propulsive stroking path.

A close-up view of Elizabeth's backstroke finish, in Figure 6.3, shows that she finishes her stroke with the same mechanics as Aaron. In Frame 1 her hand/forearm are precisely pitched and positioned to get the most forward-directing propulsion from this late stage of the pull. In Frame 2 she finishes with a straight arm, hand below hip level.

**FIGURE 6.3.** Elizabeth Beisel presses back and down, finishing the backstroke pull with a straight arm and her hand below hip level.

Once Elizabeth finishes the pull cycle, she releases her hold on the water by turning her palm perpendicular, facing her leg, as she lifts her hand/arm up for the overwater recovery phase of the stroke (Frame 3).

## BODY POSITION

The curvilinear pull pattern is more easily navigated when backstrokers position their body properly in the water.

Backstrokers position the face and chest out of the water, with the head parallel to the water line. The hips position just below the water's surface, so the legs remain in the water while kicking. Because the hips ride below the water's surface there is a slight curvature to the body rather than a rigid flat body position. Figure 6.4 shows Elizabeth and Aaron positioned with faces and chests out of the water, and hips just below the surface.

Figure 6.5 shows an elite backstroker's body position from an above-water perspective. Aaron's face and chest ride just above the surface of the water, and his hips position just below the surface. Aaron's chin is neutral—he neither

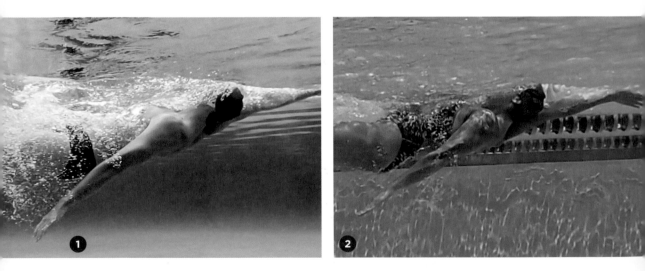

**FIGURE 6.4.** Aaron (1) and Elizabeth (2) stroke with faces and chests just above the waterline, and hips just below the surface of the water.

**FIGURE 6.5.** Aaron keeps his head steady and looks toward the sky while stroking.

tucks it in nor juts it out. He looks toward the sky. Elite backstrokers strive to maintain this head position—steady and straight –throughout the stroke cycle.

Backstrokers recover with a straight arm over the water, as Aaron does here. The shoulder, not the hand, leads the recovery and lifts the arm after the finish of the pull. The shoulder should brush by the cheek/chin as the arm passes by the head, as we see in Aaron's stroke.

## STROKE TIMING AND CORE MOVEMENT

Let's take a closer look at two other key elements in backstroke: stroke timing and core movement.

Figure 6.6 shows Aaron navigating from extension through the finish of the stroke. In Frame 1 he coordinates his arms such that his left arm enters the water at the moment his right arm finishes the stroke. We see this same arm coordination in Elizabeth's stroke in Figure 6.3. Her recovering arm does

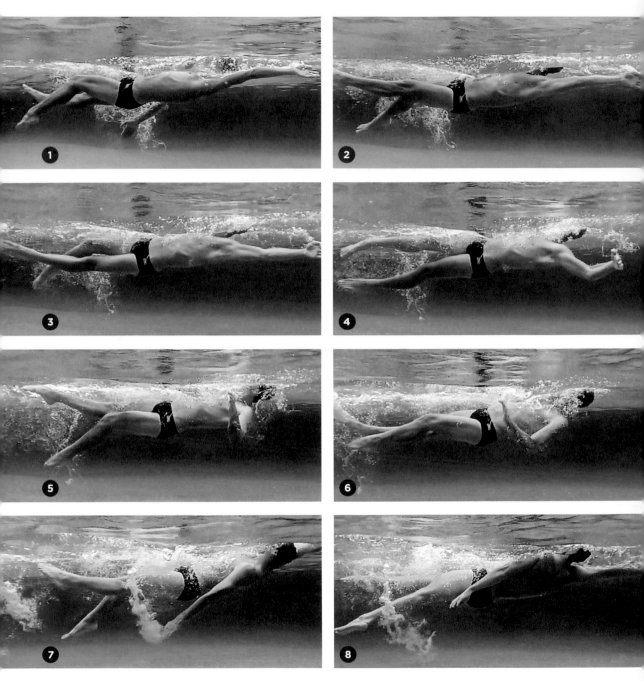

**FIGURE 6.6.** Aaron connects his kick and core movement with his pull.

not complete entry into the water until the propelling arm finishes the stroke below hip level (Frame 2). Once the recovering arm enters the water, elite backstrokers rotate their bodies toward the entering arm (also seen in Frame 3 of Elizabeth's stroke in Figure 6.3). They reach their maximal degree of rotation, which is approximately 25–30 degrees on their side, as they prepare to catch. Frames 2 and 3 of Figure 6.6 show Aaron rotating to the left as he extends and begins to catch on that arm.

Once the catch is made, elite backstrokers rotate from the hips in the other direction, as Aaron does in Frame 4. He starts rotating back to the right. During the diagonal and finish phases of the stroke, he continues the movement along the long axis to a hips-neutral position (Frames 5–7). In the final frame he completes his rotation to the right (25–30 degrees) as his right arm enters and extends in the water. Aaron says that at the finish of the stroke he feels his body compress on the side of the finishing hand/arm, and extend on the side where his hand enters the water. This adds rhythm and power to his pull.

You can also see in the last two frames that Aaron's right arm enters the water as his left arm finishes below hip level. This elite-level timing minimizes deceleration in the stroke.

## KICK TIMING

To further minimize deceleration, elite backstrokers kick 6 times per arm stroke cycle, and each beat is delivered at specific moments of the pull. Figure 6.6 shows how the beats of Aaron's kick connect with his pull.

- **Beat 1.** The left leg kicks as the left arm enters and extends (Frames 1 and 2).
- **Beat 2.** The right leg kicks as the left arm catches (Frames 3 and 4).
- **Beat 3.** The left leg kicks as the left arm moves through the diagonal and finish phases. This is the power-packed punch! (Frames 5–7).
- **Beat 4.** The right leg kicks as the left arm lifts from the water (Frame 8).
- **Beats 5 and 6.** These kicks occur as the arm recovers over the water.

**FIGURE 6.7.** Elizabeth kicks up with her right leg as she catches with her left arm.

Elizabeth connects her pull and kick just as Aaron does. Let's look at two moments in the stroke cycle when this occurs. In Figure 6.7 we see Elizabeth bend her knee in preparation for a propulsive kick with her right leg as she catches with her left arm—as Aaron does in Frame 3 of Figure 6.6.

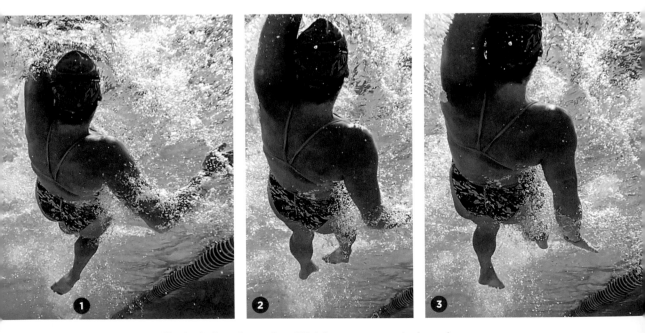

**FIGURE 6.8.** Elizabeth times her pull and kick for a power-packed punch.

**KNEE POSITION**

In this chapter's photos, notice that in Elizabeth's and Aaron's kicks, the knees do not separate far from each other. Both swimmers keep the kick narrow in terms of knee separation. This ensures their knees will not break the surface of the water. Take note in every frame that both of these world-class backstrokers' leg action occurs just below the surface of the water.

In Figure 6.8 we see that Elizabeth times her power-packed punch just as Aaron does his. She bends her right leg in Frame 1 as her right arm navigates the diagonal phase of the stroke, and the propulsive kicking action continues as she finishes the pull in Frames 2 and 3. It's a powerful Triple P.

## THE UNDERWATER DOLPHIN KICK

The underwater dolphin kick is used by elite backstrokers off the start and after each turn. Swimming rules limit the underwater kick to 15 meters, and just about every world-class backstroker approaches the edge of that line off the start. On average, elite backstrokers take approximately 9–11 dolphin kicks to reach the 13–14-meter mark; they arrive at that mark in approximately 5.5–6.0 seconds, kicking at a rate between 0.35–0.45 seconds per kick.

On turns, elite backstrokers surface sooner than they do off the start. They dolphin-kick underwater on average 3.5 seconds and surface between the 7–9-meter mark.

Figure 6.9 on the next page shows Aaron's underwater dolphin kick. He bends his knees to utilize lift and drag forces for forward thrust during the kick. Notice also how he gradually surfaces in Frames 3 and 4 as he approaches the 15-meter mark. He does not stay at one depth and then abruptly surface; rather, he angles his body and gradually ascends so as not to disrupt his forward momentum.

**FIGURE 6.9.** Aaron gradually—rather than abruptly—surfaces as he approaches the 15-meter mark so as not to disrupt his forward momentum.

## PRACTICE DRILL

One of Aaron's favorite drills is the "scull and pull," which is designed to help a swimmer feel for the catch from the extended straight-arm entry. Since backstrokers cannot see their hand/arm during entry and catch, it is useful to repeatedly practice the motion in isolation and develop the proprioceptive ability to know that the hand/arm faces back on the water.

Figure 6.10 shows Aaron doing the scull and pull. In Frame 1 his left arm enters the water straight and extended. Feeling for the catch after this straight-arm entry is the "scull" portion of the drill, as seen in Frames 2 and 3. When Aaron feels his hand/arm is positioned facing back on the water (Frame 3), he returns to the extended position, as seen in Frames 4, 5, and 6, so he can repeat the scull motion and practice feeling for the catch again. Once he has felt the catch a second time he pulls through (the "pull" portion of the drill) to the diagonal and finish phases of the stroke and switches arms.

**FIGURE 6.10.** Aaron practices his backstroke catch via the scull and pull drill.

Even a world-record holder such as Aaron continually trains to sharpen his proprioceptive ability. Incorporate this drill in your training so you can improve your own ability to feel when your hand/arm is positioned facing back on the water.

———

Remember, great mechanics are the key to fast swimming. Practice perfecting the curvilinear pull path, core movement, stroke timing, and a 6-beat kick every chance you get, and you will soon see a beautiful and fast backstroke take shape.

## STROKE DATA

### Aaron Peirsol, 2009 World Championships—Rome, Italy

**200-meter backstroke, 50-meter pool**
**Time: 1:51.92 (gold medal and world record)**

| METERS | # OF STROKES* | RATE (S/STROKE CYCLE) | SPLIT |
|--------|--------------|----------------------|-------|
| 1st 50 | 15 | 1.5 | 26.52 |
| 2nd 50 | 16 | 1.48 | 54.90 (28.38) |
| 3rd 50 | 16.5 | 1.42–1.45 | 1:23.30 (28.40) |
| 4th 50 | 18.5 | 1.30–1.35 | 1:51.92 (28.62) |

* Stroke counts listed as full stroke cycles

**START AND TURN DATA**
Time and distance underwater off start: 5.5 s, 13–14 m
Time and distance underwater off turns: 3.6–3.9 s, 9–11 m
Hand-to-feet time on turns: 1.25–1.35 s

## Missy Franklin, 2012 Olympics—London

**200-meter backstroke, 50-meter pool**
**Time: 2:04.06 (gold medal and world record)**

| METERS | # OF STROKES* | RATE (S/STROKE CYCLE) | SPLIT |
|---|---|---|---|
| 1st 50 | 17 | 1.3 | 29.53 |
| 2nd 50 | 19 | 1.4 | 1:00.50 (30.97) |
| 3rd 50 | 19.5 | 1.4 | 1:32.16 (31.66) |
| 4th 50 | 20.5 | 1.4 | 2:04.06 (31.90) |

*Stroke counts listed as full stroke cycles*

**START AND TURN DATA**
Time and distance underwater off start: 5.6 s, 12 m
Time and distance underwater off turns: 3.4 s, 7–8 m
Hand-to-feet time on turns: 1.0–1.2 s

## Elizabeth Beisel, 2012 Olympics—London

**200-meter backstroke, 50-meter pool**
**Time: 2:06.55 (bronze medal)**

| METERS | # OF STROKES* | RATE (S/STROKE CYCLE) | SPLIT |
|---|---|---|---|
| 1st 50 | 16.5 | 1.30 | 30.12 |
| 2nd 50 | 19.5 | 1.42 | 1:02.04 (31.92) |
| 3rd 50 | 20 | 1.42 | 1:34.40 (32.36) |
| 4th 50 | 20.5 | 1.37–1.40 | 2:06.55 (32.15) |

*Stroke counts listed as full stroke cycles*

**START AND TURN DATA**
Time and distance underwater off start: 6.5 s, 14 m
Time and distance underwater off turns: 3.5 s, 7–8 m
Hand-to-feet time on turns: 1.2–1.4 s

## Aaron Peirsol, 2009 U.S. National Championships

**100-meter backstroke, 50-meter pool**
**Time: 51.94 (gold medal and world record)**

| METERS | # OF STROKES* | RATE (S/STROKE CYCLE) | SPLIT |
|---|---|---|---|
| 1st 50 | 15.5 | 1.25 | 25.35 |
| 2nd 50 | 18 | 1.20–1.25 | 51.94 (26.59) |

*\* Stroke counts listed as full stroke cycles*

**START AND TURN DATA**
Time and distance underwater off start: 5.5 s, 13–14 m
Time and distance underwater off turns: 5.2 s, 11–12 m
Hand-to-feet time on turns: 1.25 s

## Elizabeth Beisel, 2014 NCAA Division I Championships

**400-yard individual medley, 25-yard pool**
**Time: 3:58.84**
**Backstroke split: 59.7**

| YARDS | # OF STROKES* | RATE (S/STROKE CYCLE) | SPLIT |
|---|---|---|---|
| 1st 25 | 6.5 | 1.6 | Not available |
| 2nd 25 | 7 | 1.6 | 30.1 |
| 3rd 25 | 7 | 1.6 | Not available |
| 4th 25 | 7 | 1.6 | 59.7 (29.6) |

*\* Stroke counts listed as full stroke cycles*

**START AND TURN DATA**
Time and distance underwater off start: n/a
Time and distance underwater off turns: 3.2–3.8 s, 7–8 yards
Hand-to-feet time on turns: 1.25–1.35 s

**SHEILA T. CLASSIC PICK**

# Rick Carey

**1983 NCAA Division I Championships**
**100-yard backstroke, 25-yard pool**
**Time: 48.25 (1st place and NCAA record)**

| YARDS | # OF STROKES* | RATE (S/STROKE CYCLE) | SPLIT |
|-------|---------------|------------------------|-------|
| 1st 25 | 7 | 1.05 | Not available |
| 2nd 25 | 9 | 1.07 | 22.93 |
| 3rd 25 | 9 | 1.07 | Not available |
| 4th 25 | 9.5 | 1.10–1.12 | 48.25 (25.32) |

* Stroke counts listed as full stroke cycles

**START AND TURN DATA**
Time and distance underwater off start: 3.85 s, 9–10 yards
Time and distance underwater off turns: 2.1–2.5 s, 6–7 yards
Hand-to-feet time on turns: 0.5 s

*Note: Pre-1992 backstrokers were required to touch the wall with their hand before turning.*

BREASTSTROKE

# 7

## BREASTSTROKE

**SWIMMING TIMES IN ALL** four strokes have steadily gotten faster throughout the decades, but none so much as in the breaststroke events. Comparing Olympic gold times between Munich 1972 and London 2012 shows a radical improvement in breaststroke that has not occurred in the other strokes.

On the men's side, the winning time at the 2012 Olympics in the 200-meter freestyle was 9.64 seconds faster than the 1972 gold medal performance. The 200-meter backstroke was 9.41 seconds faster, and the 200-meter butterfly 7.74 seconds faster.* In comparison, the gold medal time in London in the 200-meter breaststroke was an impressive 14.27 seconds faster than the winning time in Munich.

---

* Prior to September 1992, backstrokers were required to remain on their back and touch the wall with their hand before initiating the turn. Since September 1992, swimmers may roll onto their chest and take a single- or double-arm pull going into the turn. A portion of the time improvement in backstroke—an estimated 2–3 seconds in the 200—is attributed to the quicker turn today.

The women's results show a similar phenomenon. To top the podium at the 2012 Olympic Games required that women swim 9.95 seconds faster than their 1972 counterparts in the 200-meter freestyle, 11.51 seconds faster in the 200-meter butterfly, 15.13 seconds faster in the 200-meter backstroke, and a whopping 22.12 seconds faster in the 200-meter breaststroke.

Further evidence of the comparative revolution in breaststroke is seen in the U.S. Olympic Trials qualifying standards. In freestyle, backstroke, and butterfly events, the 2012 qualifying standards for both men and women have barely budged from the standards set a quarter century ago for the 1988 Olympic Trials, and in four events on the men's side the 2012 standards were actually *slower* than the 1988 standards (200-, 400-, and 1,500-meter freestyles, and 200-meter butterfly).

In breaststroke events, however, the 2012 Olympic Trials qualifying times were significantly faster than the 1988 standards. The 100-meter breaststroke qualifying time for men in 2012 was 1.3 seconds faster than the 1988 qualifying time, and the 200-meter breaststroke 3.8 seconds faster. On the women's side the 2012 cut-off time in the 100-meter breaststroke was 3.2 seconds faster, and the 200-meter standard 5.2 seconds faster, than in 1988.

Why the difference? What has happened in breaststroke that has not happened in the other strokes? The answer is that breaststroke technique has changed dramatically in recent decades. While times have improved in every stroke thanks to high-tech swimsuits, better starts and turns, and improved strength training methods, breaststroke has, in addition, experienced a major mechanical overhaul that none of the other strokes have. You could study the mechanics of the great swimmers in butterfly, backstroke, and freestyle from the 1970s and 1980s and glean nearly as much valuable technique information as you would studying the fastest swimmers in those strokes today. This is not the case with breaststroke.

Changes in breaststroke have occurred in core movement, body position, and timing in a continuing effort to minimize resistance. Breaststroke is the only stroke in which swimmers push water forward with both the arms and legs during the recovery portion of the stroke cycle, causing massive resistance and deceleration. Therefore, technique considerations often focus on minimizing resistance during these actions.

The prevailing belief in the 1970s was that to minimize resistance, swimmers should position the body as flat as possible during all phases of the stroke, lifting only the head from the water to take the breath. Figure 7.1 shows the flat-style breaststroke considered the most efficient for minimizing resistance at that time.

**FIGURE 7.1.** In the flat-style breaststroke technique of the 1970s, swimmers minimized resistance on the body but experienced significant drag on the arms as they recovered forward.

Notice the position of the swimmer's arms as they recover forward in the water. Although his body is positioned horizontally to minimize resistance, there is a significant amount of frontal drag on his arms as he pushes them forward.

Compare the 1970s form to today's form in Figure 7.2. Rebecca Soni, 2012 Olympic gold medalist, lifts her head, shoulders, and upper body from the water and recovers her arms forward from this raised position. It may seem counterintuitive to raise the body so high since swimmers want to move forward rather than up, but with the upper arms above the water, they encounter much less frontal resistance than we see in the 1970s form.

The breaststroke technique of today is challenging and vigorous—and, when done properly, blisteringly fast. We are fortunate in this chapter to be able to study the mechanics,

**FIGURE 7.2.** Rebecca Soni lifts her upper body and recovers her arms forward at the surface.

timing, and core movement of contemporary world-class elites Rebecca Soni, Laura Sogar, and Nicolas Fink.

## THE PULL AND KICK PATTERN

Minimizing resistance is critical in breaststroke, and techniques for mastering this skill will be highlighted in the chapter, but let's begin our review by looking at the curvilinear pull and kick paths that generate propulsion. The kick in breaststroke is studied as a path just like the pull is, due to its three-dimensional nature and the fact that it stands as a breaststroker's sole source of propulsion for half the stroke cycle. Breaststroke is a two-stage stroke. Athletes pull, *then* kick. They do not pull and kick simultaneously as happens in the other strokes.

Let's first look at the pulling action. Figure 7.3 shows Rebecca navigating the pull path. Breaststrokers start each stroke cycle in a streamline position with arms and head below the water surface, as Rebecca does in Frame 1. From the extended streamline position Rebecca sweeps her hands/arms out past shoulder width in Frame 2. The out-sweep is not propulsive, but it is key for establishing a strong catch position. Rebecca bends her elbows to position her hands and forearms facing back on the water to make the catch in Frames 3 and 4.

Those two frames show that Rebecca's catch is wider than we see in other strokes. Since breaststrokers pull back only to the shoulders rather than to the hips (as in the other strokes), they don't have the luxury of a long propulsive pull path. They lengthen the path by sweeping wide for the catch and pulling in a curved path *back* and *in* during the diagonal phase of the stroke. The diagonal, shown in Frames 5 and 6, is the propulsive phase of the pull. (Note: The

The velocity reached by elite breaststrokers when they kick is very similar to that reached when they pull. The arms and legs contribute equally to propulsion.

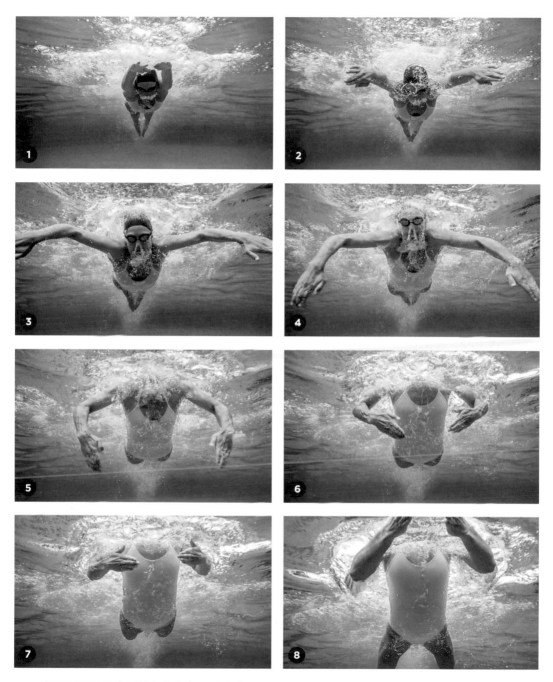

**FIGURE 7.3.** Rebecca pulls in breaststroke.

**FIGURE 7.4.** Nicolas Fink sweeps wide for the catch.

diagonal phase is called the "in-sweep" in breaststroke. *In-sweep* will be the term used throughout this chapter.)

Figure 7.4 shows that Nicolas sweeps wide, just as Rebecca does, to make the catch. From this wide position he is able to take a longer propulsive path back and in during the in-sweep phase that follows.

While looking at Frame 7 notice that Rebecca's hands and forearms approach the water surface. During the in-sweep, breaststrokers lift their head, shoulders, and upper torso from the water, which lifts their hands/forearms as well. From this raised position the upper limbs face much less frontal resistance when they recover forward (Frame 8) than if they are pushed forward underwater.

Figure 7.5 shows, from an above-water view, how Nicolas lifts his head, shoulders, and upper torso from the water during the breaststroke pull. In the last frame you can see that he has lifted high enough that his hands/forearms recover forward at the surface.

Referring back to Figure 7.3, note that Rebecca's legs streamline behind her in the first seven frames as she navigates the pull. In Frame 8, when her hands/

Set the width of your catch where you feel strong and coordinated. Do not sweep so wide that you feel pain in the shoulder tendons. Strength and range of motion for a wider catch can be built over time.

arms recover forward, we see for the first time her legs enter the picture. This is a critical detail to note and will be discussed in the upcoming section on stroke timing. Right now let's look closely at the propulsive kicking path.

## HAND ACCELERATION

Remember from Chapter 2 that developing an elite-level feel for the water requires that you increase your hand speed (and hence your hand force) as you progress through the pull cycle. Since the propulsive phase of breaststroke ends with the in-sweep, breaststrokers sweep out for the catch with constant hand velocity and increase hand speed during the in-sweep.

**FIGURE 7.5.** Nicolas lifts his head, shoulders, and upper torso from the water during the breaststroke pull. From this raised position he is able to recover his hands/arms forward at the surface (4), minimizing resistance.

## THE KICK

The breaststroke kick is the only kick of the four strokes that is three-dimensional and has a catch. To generate propulsion during the breaststroke kick, swimmers make a semicircular sweep with the feet *out*, *back*, and *down* to start the kick, and then *in*, *back*, and *down* to finish the kick.

Figure 7.6 shows Laura's kick. In Frame 1 Laura lifts her feet as close to her body as she can. The closer she brings her feet to her body, the more she lengthens the propulsive kicking path. Notice also that we barely see Laura's lower legs and feet in Frame 1, because she minimizes resistance by "hiding" the lower limbs behind the body as she lifts during the recovery.

Frame 1 also shows that Laura separates her knees approximately shoulder width apart as she sets up for the kick. The knee separation (approximately hip width) places her in a strong mechanical position to deliver power to the kick once she makes the catch.

In Frame 2 Laura flexes her feet at the ankles, so the bottoms of her feet face back on the water. At the same time, she turns her feet out, positioning them just outside her knees, and rotates her thighs in toward the midline of her body. Breaststrokers turn the upper legs *in*, while the lower legs and feet turn *out*. *This is the catch moment.* Laura is now in position to hold water with the bottoms of her feet and press back to propel herself forward.

Once Laura makes the catch, she sweeps her feet *out*, *back*, and *down*, as seen in Frames 3 and 4, and then *in*, *back*, and *down*, as seen in Frames 5 and 6. Notice that her feet and lower legs make the semicircular sweep, not her upper legs.

The breaststroke kick requires flexibility in the hip and knee joints. While training the internal rotation of the upper leg and external rotation of the lower leg, monitor knee joint health. Rotate only so far that you feel no strain on the ligaments and tendons. Just as with the catch on the arm stroke, flexibility and strength in leg rotation build over time.

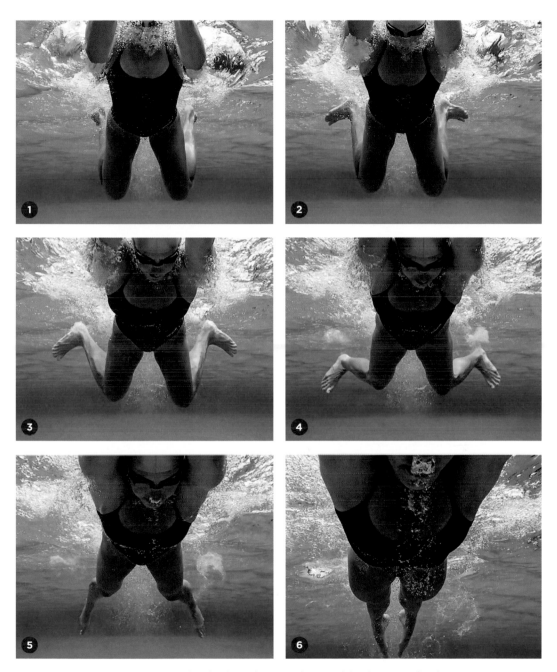

**FIGURE 7.6.** Laura Sogar pushes back on the water in a semicircular sweep for the breaststroke kick.

She maintains the same degree of knee separation throughout the kick, until she brings her legs together at the finish. Propulsion ends once the feet sweep inside shoulder width (Frame 5), but it is important to finish the kick with the feet and legs together, as we see in Frame 6, to minimize resistance.

The rear-angle perspective in Figure 7.7 shows details of Laura's kick that we could not see from a head-on view. Notice the *down* component of the

**FIGURE 7.7.** Laura keeps her ankles flexed, feet facing back on the water, as long as possible during the breaststroke kick.

three-dimensional breaststroke kick. Laura catches with her feet high in the water—near the surface—in Frame 1. As she kicks back in a semicircular sweep, her feet direct slightly *down*. She does not kick back at the surface.

The rear-angle view also shows that Laura keeps her ankles flexed (feet facing back on the water) in Frames 1–3. It's not until she nears the finish of the kick, in Frame 4, that she points her feet. The best breaststroke kickers keep their ankles flexed, feet pushing back on the water, as long as possible. It is not until the feet reach shoulder width that propulsive potential ends and the swimmer points the feet to streamline the lower limbs.

## STROKE TIMING AND CORE MOVEMENT

Breaststrokers generate great propulsion and experience rapid forward velocity when they navigate the pull and kick paths properly, but their efforts can be dampened severely if they do not incorporate elite-level technique to recover the limbs forward. In his book *Swimming Fastest*, Ernie Maglischo quantifies the extent to which deceleration can affect breaststrokers during the arm and leg recovery phase of the stroke:

> One of the most important differences between world-class and less successful breaststrokers can be attributed to this phase of the stroke cycle. World-class breaststroke swimmers decelerate less and they spend less time in this valley. The best swimmers do not decelerate much more than 1 meter/second during this time and they do not spend more than 0.30 sec in the valley. Less skilled breaststrokers will often decelerate 1.5 meters/second or more and they will spend 0.40 to 0.60 sec in the valley before completing the leg recovery. (Maglischo 2003, 229)

Elite breaststrokers minimize the severity and duration of deceleration during the arm and leg recovery by mastering techniques in core movement and stroke timing. Let's study how they do this. Figure 7.8 on the next page shows Rebecca's world-record form.

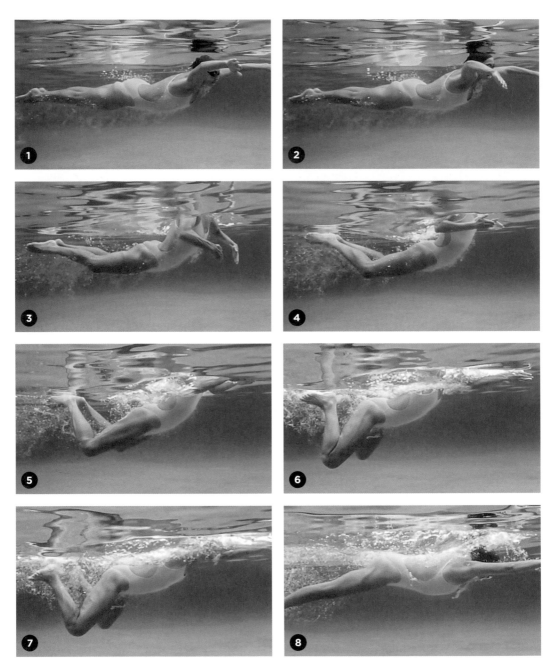

**FIGURE 7.8.** Rebecca generates propulsion with her arms and legs and minimizes resistance with sophisticated core movement and timing technique.

Rebecca navigates the catch in Frames 1 and 2, and while doing so, streamlines her torso and legs behind her. It is not until her hands reach shoulder width during the in-sweep, in Frame 3, that she begins to position for the upcoming kick. Rebecca bends her knees in Frames 3–5 to lift her feet toward her body. Notice in these frames that Rebecca does *not* flex her hips. She postpones flexing the powerful hips until Frame 6, when her feet are just a moment away from turning out for the catch (this is why we do not see Rebecca's legs until Frame 8 of Figure 7.3 on page 129). Postponing hip flexion until these last moments is important for reducing resistance, because hip flexion causes the upper legs to push forward against the water.

Rebecca is able to delay hip flexion because she lifts her body at a 45-degree angle during the in-sweep, as seen in Frames 3–5. Lifting her torso in this manner inclines her upper legs down in the water so she can bend her knees without her feet breaking the surface. Water flows past the 45-degree inclined body (Frame 5) much more smoothly than when the hips flex and push forward in the water (Frame 6). This stroking feature (delayed hip flexion via the body inclining) is another reason for the significant time drops in breaststroke over the past few decades. In the flat-style breaststroke of the 1970s, swimmers had to flex the hips much earlier in the stroke cycle to keep the feet from breaking the surface of the water as the knees bent to lift the feet. Swimmers who use the flat-style stroke experience resistance on the upper legs much sooner in the stroke cycle, and for a longer period of time, slowing their forward momentum significantly.

In Frame 6 Rebecca extends her hands/arms forward before she kicks back. Breaststrokers streamline their arms and upper body before they kick back to get maximum benefit from the propulsive leg action (just as they streamline the lower body while pulling, to get maximum benefit from the arm action). Rebecca holds the streamline position until she finishes the kick, as seen in Frame 8.

As you study Rebecca's profile photos, note that her hips are at the surface in all frames. Elite breaststrokers keep their hips high during every part of the

The valley of deceleration to which Ernie Maglischo refers is seen in Frames 4–6 of Figure 7.8. In these frames the arms and legs recover forward at the same time, causing significant resistance. It is important to move through this part of the stroke quickly. Elite breaststrokers move through this phase in a blistering 0.30 seconds. To do so they lift their feet and recover their hands/arms quickly. Work on your speed during this phase of the stroke, so you don't sit in the valley of deceleration even a tenth of a second longer than necessary.

stroke and move their core on the short axis around the hips. As with butterfly, efforts to move the core on the axis should direct forward. Elite breaststrokers feel a connection between their chest and hips. When the head and chest lift from the water during the in-sweep, the hips are pulled *forward*. Raising the upper body has great benefits already mentioned, but those benefits can be negated if swimmers incorporate the upward motion without connecting the forward drive of the hips. Pull your hips forward as you navigate the in-sweep and lift your upper body.

Similarly, when the arms recover forward and the head and upper body drop back toward the surface, as seen in Frame 6, press the chest, head, and hands forward. *Do not dive the hands down.* Notice how Rebecca's head and hands/arms direct straight forward as she presses back into the water during the kick (Frames 6–8).

## PUTTING IT ALL TOGETHER: A REAR-PROFILE VIEW

Figure 7.9 shows Rebecca's stroke from a rear-profile perspective. Study the details of the pull and kick mechanics, and take special note of the timing of knee flexion versus hip flexion in Frames 6–9. Everything that's been discussed in this chapter is included in these photos. Enjoy!

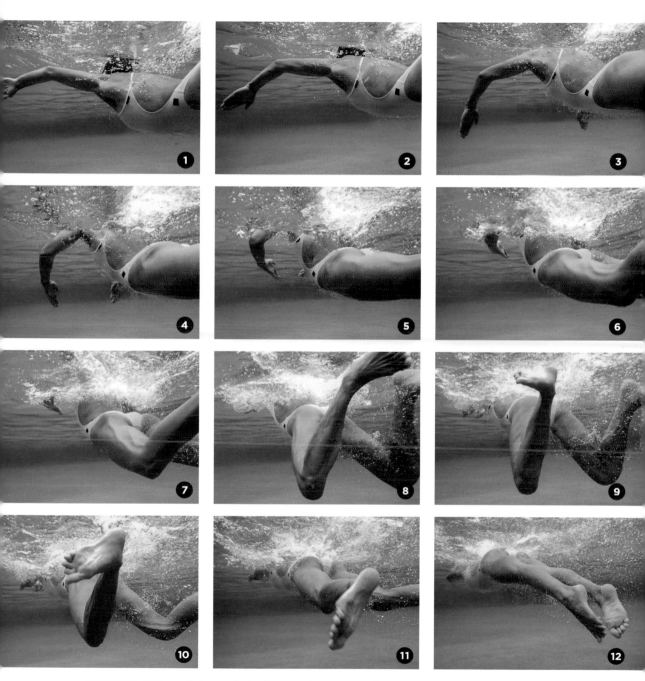

**FIGURE 7.9.** Rebecca's breaststroke from a unique perspective.

## THE PULLOUT

Swimming rules allow one breaststroke pullout after the start and each turn. The pullout is a complete stroke cycle taken underwater, with an added bonus: Swimmers may pull all the way back to the legs on the arm stroke, and they may take one butterfly kick in addition to the breaststroke kick. The pullout is of great benefit to swimmers because of the long propulsive pull path back to the legs, and because athletes stream through the deep blue, avoiding surface turbulence.

There is no limit to the distance a swimmer is allowed to travel underwater during the pullout (no 15-meter rule as in the other strokes). Most elite

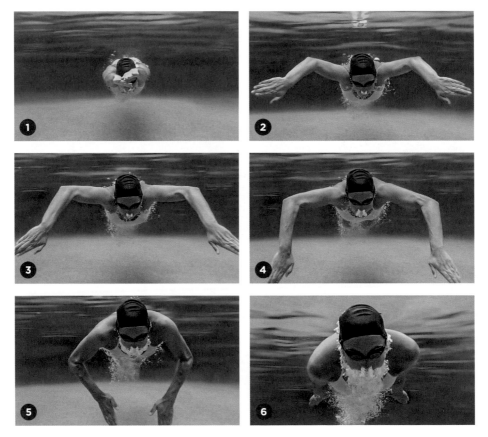

**FIGURE 7.10.** Rebecca takes a powerful pullout.

swimmers cover a distance of 8–10 meters on the pullout after the turn and surface to begin stroking in approximately 4.0–4.5 seconds.

Figure 7.10 shows Rebecca taking her pullout. After pushing off the wall and streamlining in Frame 1, she makes a beautiful catch in Frames 2–4. She navigates the diagonal phase of the pull in Frame 5 and continues pressing *back* on the water to finish the propulsive arm action at her hips/legs, as seen in Frame 6.

Rebecca must recover her arms forward from their position alongside her body. It is important that breaststrokers minimize resistance during this action. Figure 7.11 shows how Rebecca slipstreams her hands/forearms close to her body as she recovers them forward. She tucks her elbows into her sides and holds her hands/forearms in a straight horizontal line. Rebecca also directs her gaze down to keep her head from breaking its streamline position.

While the arms recover forward, the heels/feet lift toward the body and hips flex for the upcoming kick, as seen in Frame 3. Rebecca will kick to the surface and begin stroking.

**FIGURE 7.11.** Rebecca recovers her arms forward as close to her body as possible, and kicks to the surface.

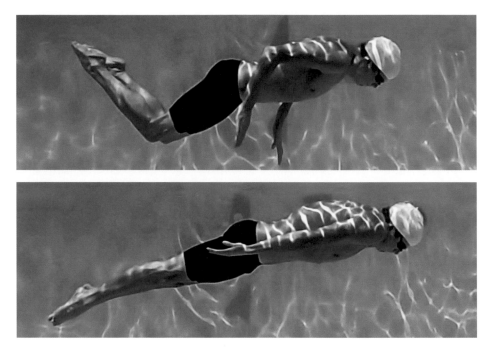

**FIGURE 7.12.** Nicolas takes his dolphin kick during the finish of the underwater arm stroke.

Breaststrokers are allowed one dolphin kick underwater at any point during the arm stroke phase of the pullout. Some elite breaststrokers take the dolphin kick during early phases of the pull while others utilize the dolphin kick during the finish phase. Figure 7.12 shows Nicolas taking his dolphin kick during the finish of his pull. You know what this means: He incorporates a power-packed punch before recovering his arms forward and kicking to the surface.

## PRACTICE DRILL

One of Laura's favorite drills is breaststroke arms with flutter kick. In this drill, swimmers pull with breaststroke arms, and flutter kick (freestyle kick) behind.

Laura likes this drill because it helps her work on her catch and helps her feel the connection between her chest and hips as she moves her core forward on the short axis. Laura also appreciates how this drill trains a fast tempo into her stroke.

To do the drill, keep a *constant, uninterrupted* flutter kick behind you during every phase of the pull. Figure 7.13 shows that Laura flutter-kicks as she extends and catches in Frames 1 and 2. She continues kicking through the in-sweep in Frames 3 and 4 and the recovery of the arms in Frames 5 and 6. Her hips remain at the surface during all phases of the pull, and she moves her core on the short axis just as she would if swimming a normal breaststroke. She lifts her head, chest, and shoulders up during the in-sweep, pulling her hips forward in the process (Frames 3 and 4), and she presses her chest back in the water during the arm recovery, directing her hands/arms straight ahead rather than diving them down (Frames 5 and 6).

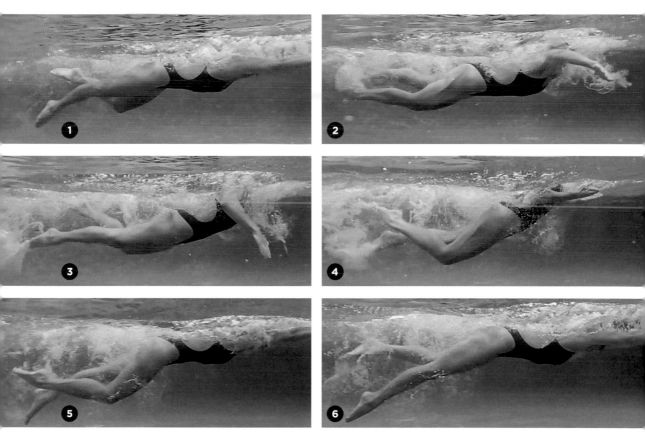

**FIGURE 7.13.** Laura does her favorite drill, breaststroke arms with flutter kick.

With the kick providing constant propulsion behind her, this drill also teaches Laura what it feels like to carry constant speed in the water, rather than succumb to the pitfalls of the valley of deceleration—when the hands recover forward. When Laura swims a normal breaststroke after doing this drill she will be highly sensitive to minimizing the degree to which she decelerates, and the duration, during her arm and leg recovery phase of the stroke.

Laura does this drill at a fast tempo. Once you master the movements, try it at a high rate of turnover. Even if you do not consider yourself a breaststroker, this drill is great for developing strong catch mechanics for any stroke.

———

Today's elite breaststrokers move in unique ways, and for good reason. Incorporate what you've learned about pull and kick mechanics, and pay special attention to minimizing the valley of deceleration during the arm/leg recovery, and you will experience the fastest breaststroke times of your life. Don't forget to work your pullouts too!

## STROKE DATA

### Nicolas Fink, 2014 NCAA Division I Championships

**100-yard breaststroke, 25-yard pool**
**Time: 51.48 (2nd place)**

| YARDS | # OF STROKES | RATE (S/STROKE CYCLE) | SPLIT |
|---|---|---|---|
| 1st 25 | 5 | 1.05 | 10.85 |
| 2nd 25 | 7 | 1.07 | 23.99 (13.14) |
| 3rd 25 | 7 | 1.07 | 37.50 (13.51) |
| 4th 25 | 8 | 1.07 | 51.48 (13.98) |

**START AND TURN DATA**
Time and distance underwater off start: 5.5 s, 15 yards
Time and distance underwater off turns: 4.4 s, 10–11 yards
Hand-to-feet time on turns: 0.75–0.85 s

## Rebecca Soni, 2012 Olympics—London

**200-meter breaststroke, 50-meter pool**
**Time: 2:19.59 (gold medal and world record)**

| METERS | # OF STROKES | RATE (S/STROKE CYCLE) | SPLIT |
|---|---|---|---|
| 1st 50 | 20 | 1.45–1.50 | 32.49 |
| 2nd 50 | 21 | 1.45 | 1:08.10 (35.61) |
| 3rd 50 | 22 | 1.35–1.40 | 1:43.95 (35.85) |
| 4th 50 | 26 | 1.25 (1.15 last 15–20 meters) | 2:19.59 (35.64) |

**START AND TURN DATA**
Time and distance underwater off start: 5.7 s, 10–11 m
Time and distance underwater off turns: 3.8–4.1 s, 7–8 m
Hand-to-feet time on turns: 0.85–0.95 s

## Laura Sogar, 2013 NCAA Division I Championships

**200-yard breaststroke, 25-yard pool**
**Time: 2:05.41 (1st place)**

| YARDS | # OF STROKES | RATE (S/STROKE CYCLE) | SPLIT |
|---|---|---|---|
| 1st 50 | 12 | 1.45–1.50 | 27.99 |
| 2nd 50 | 14 | 1.45–1.50 | 59.68 (31.69) |
| 3rd 50 | 16 | 1.35 | 1:31.88 (32.20) |
| 4th 50 | 18 | 1.30 | 2:05.41 (33.53) |

**START AND TURN DATA**
Time and distance underwater off start: 5.7 s, 12 yards
Time and distance underwater off turns: 4.0–4.1 s, 8–9 yards
Hand-to-feet time on turns: 0.90–0.95 s

*Note: Stroke counts per 25 yards: 5, 7, 7, 7, 8, 8, 8, 10*

## Cameron Van Der Burgh, 2012 Olympics—London

**100-meter breaststroke, 50-meter pool**
**Time: 58.46 (gold medal and world record)**

| METERS | # OF STROKES | RATE (S/STROKE CYCLE) | SPLIT |
|---|---|---|---|
| 1st 50 | 18 | 1.2 | 27.07 |
| 2nd 50 | 24 | 1.10–1.15 | 58.46 (31.39) |

**START AND TURN DATA**

Time and distance underwater off start: 5.0 s, 14 m
Time and distance underwater off turns: 4.2 s, 9 m
Hand-to-feet time on turns: 0.85 s

## Rebecca Soni, 2009 World Championships—Rome, Italy

**100-meter breaststroke, 50-meter pool**
**Time: 1:04.84 (gold medal and world record)**

| METERS | # OF STROKES | RATE (S/STROKE CYCLE) | SPLIT |
|---|---|---|---|
| 1st 50 | 22 | 1.18 | 31.03 |
| 2nd 50 | 24 | 1.18–1.22 | 1:04.84 (33.81) |

**START AND TURN DATA**

Time and distance underwater off start: 5.0 s, 10 m
Time and distance underwater off turns: 4.3 s, 8 m
Hand-to-feet time on turns: 0.93 s

**SHEILA T. CLASSIC PICK**

# Penny Heynes, 1996 Olympics—Atlanta, Georgia

**100-meter breaststroke, 50-meter pool**

**Time: 1:07.73 (gold medal)**

| METERS | #OF STROKES | RATE (S/STROKE CYCLE) | SPLIT TIME |
|---|---|---|---|
| 1st 50 | 22 | 1.20 | 31.65 |
| 2nd 50 | 27 | 1.10 | 1:07.73 (36.08) |

**START AND TURN DATA**

Time and distance underwater off start: 5.5 s, 10 m

Time and distance underwater off turns: 3.7 s, 7 m

Hand-to-feet time on turns: 0.95 s

# FREESTYLE

**IN FREESTYLE EVENTS,** swimmers are *free* to swim any *style* they choose. There are no rules governing the stroking motion, as there are in butterfly, backstroke, and breaststroke. Swimmers can move, position, twist, and torque their body and limbs however they wish.

Freedom equates to speed. The world records in freestyle events are on average 5 seconds faster per 100 meters than they are in butterfly and backstroke events, and 12 seconds faster per 100 meters than breaststroke events.

Yet, with all this freedom, elite freestylers, from sprinters to distance swimmers, use the same stroke, one that is to date considered the fastest way to move a human body through water: alternating arms with a scissors kick, body positioned on the chest, and core rotation on the long axis.

Along with freedom, freestyle offers variety. Butterfly, backstroke, and breaststroke have only two individual races each at the Olympics (the 100-meter and 200-meter events), but freestyle offers seven individual events—the 50-, 100-, 200-, 400-, 800-, and 1,500-meter races in the pool, and the 10K race in open water.

There is something for every swimmer when it comes to freestyle. In this chapter we will look at the technique of athletes who have topped the international ranks in the pool and open water in middle distance to distance events (the 200-meter to 10K)—Ashley Whitney, Peter Vanderkaay, and Andrew Gemmell. In Appendix B we will look at the "straight-arm" variation of freestyle technique as we review the stroke of the fastest man ever to take to water—sprinter Vladimir Morozov.

---

**FREESTYLE RULES**

Three rules must be followed in freestyle events; none pertain to how a swimmer moves the body and limbs:

1. Some part of the swimmer must touch the wall at the end of each length.

2. Some part of the swimmer must break the surface of the water throughout the race (except during the first 15 meters the swimmer may be submerged).

3. Swimmers may not do butterfly, backstroke, or breaststroke during the freestyle leg of an individual medley race or a medley relay race (swimmers may do butterfly, backstroke, or breaststroke in a freestyle event).

---

## THE PULL PATTERN

Athletes may be at liberty to move their limbs any way they choose in freestyle; however, the curvilinear pull pattern featured here is one navigated by all elite middle-distance to long-distance freestylers.

Figure 8.1 shows Peter stroking with his right arm from extension to the finish of the stroke. In Frame 1 he extends his right arm overhead, directly in front of his shoulder, before tending to the catch details in Frames 2 and 3. Frame 3 shows that when Peter is in full catch mode, his upper arm is set wide

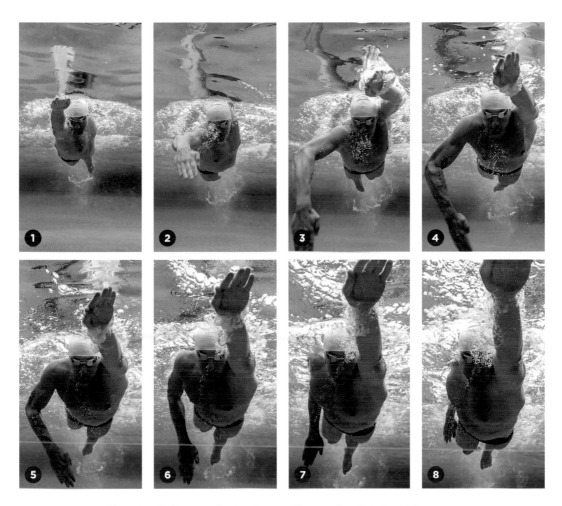

**FIGURE 8.1.** Peter Vanderkaay navigates the curvilinear pull path in freestyle.

of shoulder width, his elbow is bent and directs *up*, and his hand and forearm face back on the water.

Peter ensures the back-facing orientation of the limb as he moves through the diagonal phase in Frames 4 and 5, and the finish phase in Frames 6–8. Notice how Peter adjusts the pitch of his hand as he transitions to the diagonal between Frames 3 and 4 and then to the finish between Frames 5 and 6. The pitch is slight, but important, as it guides the limb to an adjacent plane of still water and lengthens the propulsive stroking path, all the while ensuring the resultant force of lift and drag can be used to propel him forward.

Also notice Peter's elbow during the catch in Frames 2 and 3 as compared to the diagonal phase in Frames 4 and 5. The elbow directs slightly *up* during the catch, and *out* during the diagonal phase of the stroke.

A close-up of Ashley's stroke, in Figure 8.2, shows the same mechanics. She directs her elbow *up* during the catch in Frame 1, and *out* during the diagonal in Frame 2. Note that Ashley's hand pitch in Frame 2 is the same as Peter's (Frame 4 of Figure 8.1) as she navigates the diagonal phase of the stroke. Both the upper arm and the hand are actively involved in directing an elite-level curvilinear pull path.

**FIGURE 8.2.** Ashley Whitney directs her elbow up for the catch (1) and out for the diagonal (2).

Referring back to Figure 8.1, Peter finishes the propulsive pull path near his hip (Frames 7 and 8). It is difficult to see from a head-on perspective that Peter does not straighten his arm during the finish of the stroke but rather keeps it

**FIGURE 8.3.** Andrew Gemmell keeps his arm bent as he finishes the stroke in freestyle.

bent as he presses back. The above-water perspective in Figure 8.3 offers a clearer look at this bent-arm position at the finish. Andrew's elbow is bent as he presses back with his hand/forearm and lifts his upper arm from the water during the finish phase of the stroke.

---

### HAND ACCELERATION

Remember from Chapter 2 that developing an elite-level feel for the water requires that you increase your hand speed (and hence your hand force) as you progress through the pull cycle. Hand speed is slowest during the catch and fastest at the finish of the stroke. Elite swimmers accelerate water back at the finish of the stroke.

---

## STROKE TIMING AND CORE MOVEMENT

Elite freestylers also time their arms and drive the core on the long axis in near-identical fashion. Figure 8.4 shows Peter's stroke timing and core movement throughout the stroke cycle.

In Frame 1 Peter extends the right arm forward as the left arm finishes the pull cycle (left arm not visible). Notice that his hips rotate up on the left side to follow the momentum of the finishing arm, but his right arm, shoulder, and upper torso extend forward. The right side of the body is charged fully with the task of making the catch, so it extends rather than rotates.

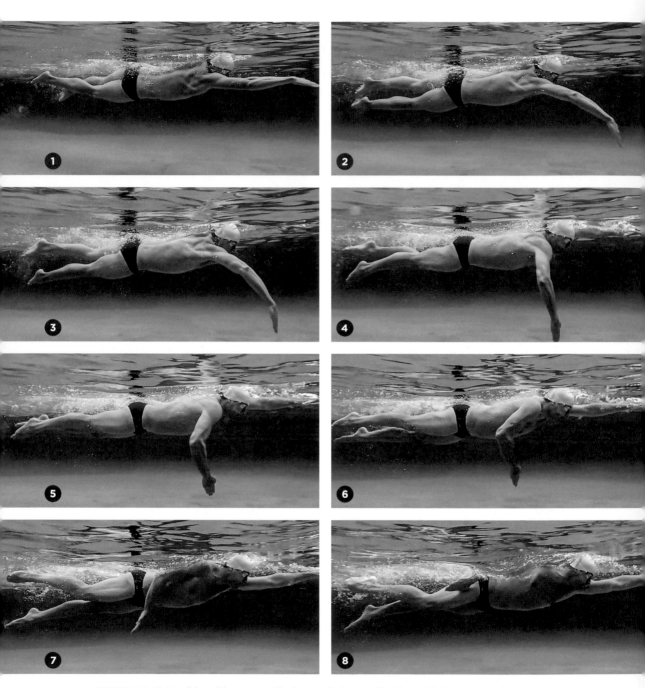

**FIGURE 8.4.** Peter drives his core on the long axis in coordination with the arm stroke.

Frame 2 shows that as Peter begins positioning the right hand/forearm to face back on the water for the catch, his hips begin to rotate the other direction. Hip rotation starts as the catch takes shape. Peter's hips continue to rotate on the long axis as he progresses through the phases of the stroke, as shown through to Frame 8. Hip rotation on the long axis always follows the momentum of the arm pull.

This figure also allows us to see the timing of the arms in an elite freestyler's stroke. In Frame 3 Peter is in the thick of the catch phase of the pull cycle. His hand/forearm faces directly back on the water. We also see his left hand enter the water in this frame. Swimming terminology calls this moment in the stroke cycle "front-quadrant swimming." Both arms are overhead—in the front quadrant of the stroke—as opposed to being in the rear quadrant near the hips/legs. Swimmers must be strong in their upper core to balance on the long axis when working in the front quadrant.

Figure 8.5 shows from a head-on view Peter's and Ashley's core strength and arm timing during this front-quadrant moment in the stroke cycle. The right

**FIGURE 8.5.** Peter (1) and Ashley (2) balance their core on the long axis as their arms pass by each other, moving in opposite directions, in the front quadrant.

arm is in full catch mode when the left hand enters the water (Ashley's fingertips can just be seen entering the water). Both arms are overhead, moving in opposite directions, and there is a mild diagonal twist to the core, not a tipping of the body on its side. It takes strength to balance the torso on the long axis as the two arms move in opposite directions overhead.

Referring back to Figure 8.4, Frames 4–8 show that once the arms pass each other in the front quadrant, Peter progresses through the diagonal and finish phases of the stroke with his right arm and extends his left arm forward at the surface.

---

### ONE GIANT STROKING PADDLE

In Figure 8.4 look closely at the position of Peter's forearm in relation to his hand. Peter's wrist is always straight, and his hand/forearm held in line, in every frame. He uses his limb as one giant stroking paddle to press against lift and drag forces.

---

## THE KICK

The number of kicks per stroke cycle in freestyle varies from swimmer to swimmer. Athletes connect either a 2-beat, 4-beat, or 6-beat kick with their stroke. Two-beat kickers kick twice (once on each leg) per full stroke cycle, and 6-beat kickers kick 6 times (3 beats per leg) during a full stroke cycle. The more kicks per stroke cycle, the more propulsion the legs provide.

The 6-beat kick is imperative for reaching top speeds. Swimmers who aspire to race among the elite ranks in sprint events (the 50 and 100) cannot survive the heat of battle without it. The vast majority of middle-distance swimmers (200 and 400) utilize the 6-beat kick as well, and although some distance swimmers (800, 1,500, and open-water 10K) save energy by using the less propulsive 2-beat or 4-beat kick for a portion of their race, the best among them know exactly when and how to incorporate a 6-beat kick into their stroke when fast gears are required.

Open-water swimmers should know how to incorporate a 6-beat kick into their stroke to get out of the fray at the beginning of the race, bridge a gap that may form during the middle of a race, or sprint to the finish. Athletes who do not know how to do so will be left behind by those who have the ability to kick into higher gears.

Regardless of whether a swimmer uses a 2-, 4-, or 6-beat kick, there is one beat that all freestylers share—the power-packed punch. Figure 8.6 shows Peter's Triple P. He kicks down with his right leg as his right hand finishes the stroke and lifts from the water.

**FIGURE 8.6.** Peter kicks down with his right leg as his right hand finishes the pull for a power-packed punch.

> ### TIMING THE BEATS OF THE 6-BEAT KICK
>
> The beats of the 6-beat kick occur at specific moments in the stroke cycle. Below is a review of when each kick takes place:
>
> **Beat 1:** The left leg kicks as the right arm extends.
>
> **Beat 2:** The right leg kicks as the right arm catches.
>
> **Beat 3:** The left leg kicks as the right arm moves through the diagonal.
>
> **Beat 4:** The power-packed punch—right leg kicks as right arm finishes.
>
> **Beats 5 and 6:** The left leg kicks, then right leg, as arm recovers over water.
>
> The cycle starts over when the right arm extends for the next stroke.
>
> You can see the 6-beat timing in the photos in this chapter, as well as in Vladimir Morozov's stroke in Appendix B. All swimmers are encouraged to learn the timing of the 6-beat kick, including distance swimmers, open-water swimmers, and triathletes, so that when faster speeds are needed during a race, athletes are able to go into a higher gear.

## BREATHING

Some elite swimmers breathe to just one side, while others alternate and breathe on both sides. It is not important whether you breathe to one side or both; what is important is that you do the technique correctly.

Taking the breath is a combination of turning the head and rotating the core on the long axis. Figure 8.7 shows Ashley taking a breath to her right. In Frame 1 she makes the catch with her right arm, and her head is neutral; she is not yet turning for the breath. In Frames 2–4 Ashley gradually turns her head to the right as she moves through the diagonal and finish phases of the stroke. Notice the complementary core rotation as well. She times the breath with her core movement to the right.

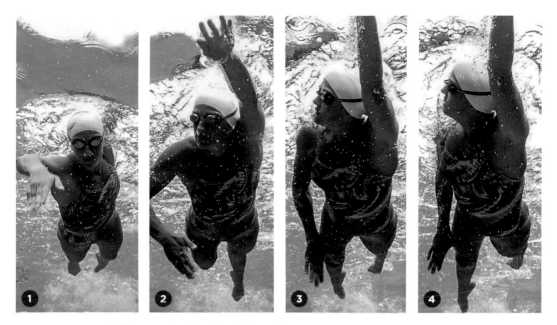

**FIGURE 8.7.** Ashley turns her head in timing with core rotation to take a breath.

Figure 8.8 shows Ashley taking in air from an above-water perspective. Notice that she does not lift her head up. Her head lays flat in the water as she simply turns to the side. There is no need to lift the head for the breath, because a small pocket of air forms near the mouth from the wake of the water.

**FIGURE 8.8.** Ashley takes a breath as her arm navigates the finish phase of the stroke.

**FIGURE 8.9.** Ashley takes a breath to the left and returns her head to the water as her left arm recovers forward.

After taking the breath, the head turns back to the water as the core rotates in the other direction and the arm on the breathing side recovers forward, seen in Ashley's stroke in Figure 8.9.

In every photo in this section on breathing, notice that Ashley maintains perfect stroke mechanics when she breathes. By maintaining her mechanics, the breath does not hinder her forward velocity.

## PRACTICE DRILL

One of Peter's favorite drills is "catch-up." He uses the drill to practice positioning his hand/arm for the catch, which helps him time the stroke properly. Having the discipline to position the limb before pressing back on the water is an important factor in developing the front-quadrant timing studied earlier in this chapter. The catch-up drill exaggerates this aspect of the stroke. It is a drill that reminds swimmers not to pull back immediately when the hand enters the water, but rather to position the limb overhead for the catch.

To do the drill, swim normal freestyle, but hold the hand/arm that is extending forward (overhead) in its extended position until the other arm completes its stroke cycle and "catches up" to the extending hand/arm. Once the stroking limb meets the waiting limb, move through the catch details with the waiting arm, and pull through. Alternate arms as you swim the length of the pool. Your primary focus during catch-up is to position the limb before pressing back.

Figure 8.10 shows Peter doing the drill. In Frame 1 he holds his right arm in an extended position overhead until his left arm finishes its stroke cycle and meets up with the right. In Frame 2 he focuses on, and makes, a beautiful catch with the right arm. Notice that his arm is quite a distance overhead as he

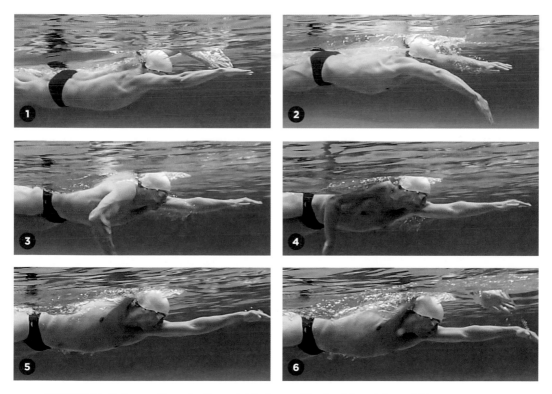

**FIGURE 8.10.** Peter positions for the catch before pulling back in catch-up drill.

makes the catch. He doesn't pull back while positioning the limb. This is critical for elite stroke timing. Frames 3 and 4 show that Peter pulls through after the catch, and his left arm waits in an extended position until the right meets up with it in Frame 6, after which Peter will work on catch mechanics and pull through with his left arm.

Catch-up drill also helps athletes build strength in the upper core by making them balance on the long axis while the arms work in the front quadrant. Notice in Frames 1, 2, and 6 how controlled and strong Peter holds his upper core to balance on the long axis as the arms work overhead. He never tips on his side. He rotates his hips, but his extending arm (the right arm in Frame 1, and the left arm in Frame 6) stays to the side of his cheek/chin, providing a stable, balanced platform.

Catch-up drill is a classic. I don't know an elite swimmer who doesn't include this one in their stable of drills. Incorporate it into your training with great purpose—to develop your catch mechanics, stroke timing, and core strength/balance.

—

In this chapter we have seen how the best in the world choose to move their limbs and body with the freedom they are given in the freestyle stroke; but remember, ultimately, you are at liberty to make your way to the other end of the pool any way you want (save the few rules highlighted in the sidebar on page 150). Feel free to think outside the box! This is the way great things happen, such as what we will see in Vladimir Morozov's stroke in Appendix B. Lift and drag forces are at your disposal. Have fun!

# STROKE DATA

## Chase Kalisz, 2014 NCAA Division I Championships

400-yard individual medley, 25-yard pool
Time: 3:34.50 (NCAA and American record)
Freestyle split: 50.93

| YARDS | # OF STROKES* | RATE (S/STROKE CYCLE) | SPLIT |
|---|---|---|---|
| 1st 25 | 7.5 | 1.35 | Not available |
| 2nd 25 | 7.5 | 1.35 | 25.77 |
| 3rd 25 | 8 | 1.35 | Not available |
| 4th 25 | 8 | 1.35 | 50.93 (25.16) |

* Stroke counts listed as full stroke cycles

### START AND TURN DATA

Time and distance underwater off start: N/A
Time and distance underwater off turns: 1.7 s, 5 yards
Hand-to-feet time on turns: 1.1–1.5 s

## Missy Franklin, 2014 NCAA Division I Championships

4 × 200-yard freestyle relay, 25-yard pool
Relay split: 1:40.08

| YARDS | # OF STROKES* | RATE (S/STROKE CYCLE) | SPLIT |
|---|---|---|---|
| 1st 50 | 14 | 1.2 | 23.01 |
| 2nd 50 | 15.5 | 1.3 | 48.39 (25.38) |
| 3rd 50 | 16 | 1.3 | 1:14.40 (26.01) |
| 4th 50 | 16.5 | 1.25 | 1:40.08 (25.68) |

* Stroke counts listed as full stroke cycles

### START AND TURN DATA

Time and distance underwater off start (relay pickup): 3.0 s, 10 yards
Time and distance underwater off turns: 2.2 s, 6 yards
Hand-to-feet time on turns: 0.90–1.20 s

*Note: Stroke counts per 25 yards: 6, 8, 7.5, 8, 8, 8, 8, 8.5*

## Peter Vanderkaay, 2008 Olympics—Beijing, China

**4 × 200-meter freestyle relay, 50-meter pool**
**Relay split: 1:44.68 (gold medal and world record)**

| METERS | # OF STROKES* | RATE (S/STROKE CYCLE) | SPLIT |
|---|---|---|---|
| 1st 50 | 14 | 1.55 | |
| 2nd 50 | 15 | 1.55 | |
| 3rd 50 | 16.5 | 1.4 | |
| 4th 50 | 17.5 | 1.35–1.38 | 1:44.68 |

* *Stroke counts listed as full stroke cycles*

**START AND TURN DATA**
Time and distance underwater off start (relay pickup): 3.6 s, 11 m
Time and distance underwater off turns: 2.8 s, 8 m
Hand-to-feet time on turns: 1.10 s

## Allison Schmitt, 2012 Olympic Games—London

**200-meter freestyle, 50-meter pool**
**Time: 1:53.61 (gold medal and Olympic record)**

| METERS | # OF STROKES* | RATE (S/STROKE CYCLE) | SPLIT |
|---|---|---|---|
| 1st 50 | 16.5 | 1.35–1.40 | 27.18 |
| 2nd 50 | 18 | 1.35–1.40 | 55.38 (28.20) |
| 3rd 50 | 19 | 1.35 | Not available |
| 4th 50 | 20 | 1.35 | 1:53.61 |

* *Stroke counts listed as full stroke cycles*

**START AND TURN DATA**
Time and distance underwater off start: 4.1 s, 10 m
Time and distance underwater off turns: 2.7 s, 7 m
Hand-to-feet time on turns: 1.10–1.30 s

## Nathan Adrian, 2012 Olympics—London

**100-meter freestyle, 50-meter pool**
**Time: 47.52 (gold medal)**

| METERS | # OF STROKES* | RATE (S/STROKE CYCLE) | SPLIT |
|---|---|---|---|
| 1st 50 | 16.5 | 1.15–1.20 | 22.64 |
| 2nd 50 | 19 | 1.15–1.20 | 47.52 (24.88) |

* Stroke counts listed as full stroke cycles

**START AND TURN DATA**
Time and distance underwater off start: 3.4 s, 11 m
Time and distance underwater off turns: 2.5 s, 7 m
Hand-to-feet time on turns: 1.05 s

**SHEILA T. CLASSIC PICK**

## Mark Spitz, 1972 Olympics—Munich, West Germany

**100-meter freestyle, 50-meter pool**
**Time: 51.22 (gold medal and world record)**

| METERS | # OF STROKES* | RATE (S/STROKE CYCLE) | SPLIT |
|---|---|---|---|
| 1st 50 | 19 | 1.10–1.15 | Not available |
| 2nd 50 | 22.5 | 1.10–1.15 | 51.22 |

* Stroke counts listed as full stroke cycles

**START AND TURN DATA**
Time and distance underwater off start: 2.5 s, 7 m
Time and distance underwater off turns: 1.0 s, 3–4 m
Hand-to-feet time on turns: Not available

# CONCLUSION

## ADOPTING ELITE TECHNIQUE

**IF, AFTER REVIEWING** the chapters in this book, you wonder whether it is even possible to incorporate the technique of the best swimmers in the world into your own stroke, I'm happy to tell you that the answer is most definitely yes. The technique you see in elite swimmers' strokes is fundamental at its heart. It is the technique that coaches on pool decks all over the world teach, whether it be to a summer league team of 6-year-old beginners, a year-round competitive age-group team, or a masters team that includes beginners and veteran swimmers. The top swimmers in the world just happen to be the ideal models for us all, because they do the fundamentals extremely well.

This is not to say that mastering what you see will be easy. Following are a few things to keep in mind as you take what you've learned from this book to the pool:

- **Range of motion.** You may lack the range of motion that elite swimmers have, especially if you have just started swimming or are older or muscle-bound. Don't worry if you lack the full range. Work within your limits. While range of motion helps, you can still function on the spectrum of proper technique with less flexibility. Many elite swimmers take yoga and Pilates classes to increase flexibility and strength. Consider taking those classes, or design your own stretching program if you feel additional range will help you master a particular motion.

- **Simple versus complex movements.** Some aspects of the stroke will be more difficult to adopt than others. Making simple mechanical adjustments to your stroke, such as incorporating a straight-arm—rather than a bent-arm—recovery in the backstroke, is manageable on the first session and should become part of your permanent stroke memory within a few weeks. However, the more complex aspects of technique, such as connecting the arms, legs, and core for that impeccable timing we see in the best swimmers' strokes, are a different story. These require more time and fortitude. Don't give up on the more complex aspects of the stroke if they don't happen right away though. Keep at it; your efforts will pay off.

- **The frequency of reinforcing technique.** Keep in mind that in all strokes you will complete one stroke cycle every 1.0 to 2.5 seconds (1.0 for fast swimming, 2.5 for easy swimming); therefore, any change you wish to adopt is either being reinforced every 1.0 to 2.5 seconds or not. Don't let this overwhelm you. Look at it as an opportunity to hone great technique every second or two. Remember also that stroke drills are designed to make this process manageable. Many drills are best done at rates as slow as 3–4 seconds per cycle, or even slower if need be to do the motion correctly.

- **Prerequisites.** It may be necessary to develop one part of the stroke before moving on to others. If you read my first book, *Swim Speed Secrets,* then you know I am big fan of developing the underwater pull pattern first. I won't tell you what to work on here, but do keep in mind that if something in your stroke does not feel right, then the underlying cause may reside in another part of your technique. (P.S. Check the pull pattern.)

- **Base level of conditioning and strength.** Each person who reads this book is at a unique point in their swimming career and overall physical health. If you are starting back on the road to fitness after years of inactivity, then you may first need to build a base level of conditioning and strength before you can expect to swim with good form. Even Olympian Rowdy Gaines says that maintaining strength is critical to his ability to hold the water. At age 54, he finds that lifting weights for 20 minutes a few times per week helps him maintain resemblance of his peak form.

- **Mentality and commitment.** Making stroke improvements depends on your commitment to the change and your focus during practice. Mastering a stroke change is as much a mental effort as it is a physical effort. When elite athletes come across valuable information, they hold onto it like a dog that won't let go of a good bone. They own the information and rarely need their coach to remind them of it. On top of all this, they recognize that good things do not happen overnight; they are patient and suffer through awkward stages of stroke development in order to reap the benefits down the road. A great mental attitude—and deliberate mindset—will do more to boost your swimming progress than anything else.

Three words nicely sum up what is required to begin the journey toward stroking like a champion: *focus*, *strength*, and *fortitude*.

We don't need to be superheroes to emulate the technique of the top swimmers. Great form is within everyone's grasp. Even for those who swim for fun or exercise only, it is perfectly reasonable for you to work on the form you see in this book. You'll discover ways of moving in three dimensions you never knew existed, and you may find that you have an aptitude for a stroke you've never tried before.

I hope you are inspired and informed by the strokes of the elite athletes photographed in this book. Practice purposefully and deliberately to adopt their form, and you will be on your way to mastering this complex sport.

# APPENDIX A
# SIGHTING TECHNIQUE FOR
# OPEN-WATER EVENTS

Open-water swimmers must navigate long distances in lakes, rivers, or oceans without the luxury of lane lines or black tiled lines below to guide them on a straight course. They rely on large, brightly colored buoys that delineate the race course at open-water swimming events, or a landmark on shore that serves as a guiding point when they train. In either case, the swimmer must lift their head from the water to sight the buoy or landmark.

Lifting the head from the water can interrupt the fluidity of the swim stroke if done incorrectly, and when athletes sense such an interruption, they tend to sight less often. They rely on bubbles from the feet of the swimmer in front of them, or assume they are going in a straight-enough line. Both of these decisions run a high risk that the athlete will swim off course, adding unnecessary meters to their already long swim.

To swim in as straight a line as possible from buoy to buoy and not interrupt the fluidity of the swim stroke, athletes must do two things:

- Sight often (even when drafting behind another swimmer).
- Sight with elite-level technique.

Elite open-water swimmers sight every 4–6 full arm-stroke cycles. Even those who have the most balanced strokes and who swim in a straight line easily in a pool will veer off course in open water within a few strokes due to waves, currents, general chop, and slight stroke imbalances. By sighting frequently, athletes make minute adjustments to their course before angling the wrong direction. Elite swimmers even sight regularly when they draft behind other swimmers, to ensure the leaders are taking the most direct route, and because water conditions and turbulence from the other competitors cause a "washing machine" effect that can push athletes from their drafting position within a few stroke cycles.

Elite swimmers are able to sight often without negatively affecting their velocity because they incorporate the sighting motion seamlessly with a breath. The proper technique for sighting is to lift the head for the sight, and then turn for the breath. The timing and technique that was reviewed for normal freestyle breathing in the freestyle chapter remains the same. The sighting action occurs in the moments before the breathing action.

Figure A.1 shows Andrew Gemmell sighting and then rolling into a breath on his right side. The photos were taken in a pool to show the technique clearly; athletes incorporate this same technique in open water. As Andrew extends and catches with his right arm in Frames 1–3, he lifts his head to sight. He lifts only so high that his eyes come out of the water. There is no need to lift the head higher, since the breath is not taken during the sighting action. Athletes keep the chin in the water while sighting so the hips do not sink.

The breath is taken after the sight. Frames 4 and 5 show that Andrew seamlessly flows into the breathing action to his right after lifting for the sight. The timing of the breath is identical to the timing studied in the freestyle chapter. Andrew turns his head to the right, as he rotates on the long axis to the right, and as his right arm navigates the back half of the stroke.

In Frame 6, Andrew returns his head to the water as his arm recovers forward overwater, just as he would if taking a normal freestyle breath.

**FIGURE A.1.** World championships open-water medalist and Olympian Andrew Gemmell sights and then seamlessly rolls into a breath.

Figure A.2 shows that Ashley Whitney employs the same sighting/breathing mechanics as Andrew. She sights as her right arm extends and catches (Frames 1 and 2), and then lays her head back down as she turns to the right for the breath (Frames 3 and 4).

**FIGURE A.2.** Ashley Whitney lifts only her eyes from the water for the sight (1 and 2). There is no need to lift higher, since the breath is taken to the side after the sighting action (3 and 4).

In Figure A.3 we can see Ashley sighting into a breath on her left side from an underwater perspective. She lifts only her eyes from the water. Her body position is not affected by this minimal lifting action, as evidenced by the fact that her hips are at the surface in all frames.

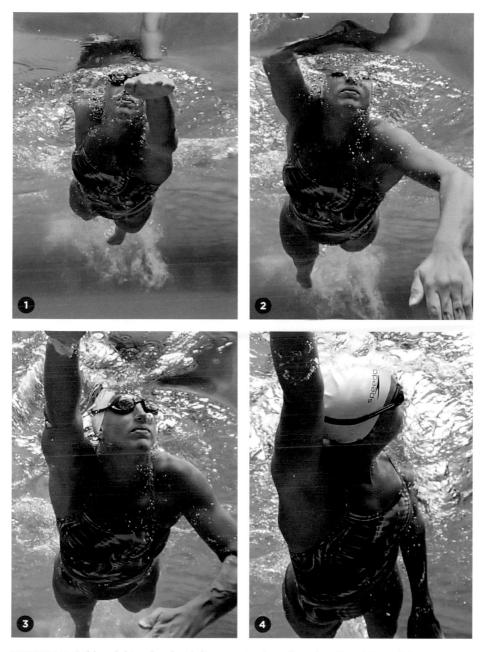

**FIGURE A.3.** Ashley sights when her left arm extends and catches (1 and 2), and then seamlessly rolls into a breath on her left side as she navigates the back half of the stroke (3 and 4).

In very wavy/choppy conditions you may need to lift the head slightly higher to see a buoy or landmark, but when doing so, consciously keep the hips at the surface. Better yet, try to time the sight when on the crest of a wave. You may have to sight two or three strokes in a row to hit the crest, but you will be quicker doing this than going off course or stopping and using a breaststroke arm action to keep your head above water to see the buoy.

And of course, do not forgo stroke mechanics when sighting. Ashley makes an elite-level catch even when she sights, as seen in Figure A.4.

**FIGURE A.4.** Ashley makes an elite-level catch even when she sights.

Practice your sighting technique in the pool once per week by doing 500–800 yards/meters, sighting twice per 25. This will hone your technique and strengthen your neck for the action, and you'll be prepared to navigate a straight course once you hit the open water.

# APPENDIX B
# SPRINT FREESTYLE:
# STRAIGHT-ARM TECHNIQUE

When Vladimir Morozov swam 17.86 for the 50-yard freestyle during his leg of the 200-yard freestyle relay at the 2013 NCAA Championships, he arguably became the fastest man ever to move through water. Those who witnessed the relay race, as well as his 40.76 100-yard freestyle (individual event), said it looked as though he was swimming atop the water rather than through it.

What does the fastest man in water do to generate such speed? Vladimir uses a straight-arm technique. Throughout the book we have seen how elite swimmers use their hand/forearm as a large paddle to maximize the surface area upon which the propulsive forces of lift and drag act. What if that paddle could be expanded even further, and include the surface area of the upper arm? How much additional power could a swimmer generate? The answer: 17.86 for a 50-yard freestyle level of power.

Many people believe the straight-arm technique refers only to the over-water recovery portion of the stroke. It is true that elite sprinters who use the straight arm technique recover their arm overwater in a straight, rather than bent-elbow, position, but it is the straight-arm position underwater, during the catch, that is the most challenging aspect to master with this specialized sprint technique.

More and more elite sprinters are adopting the straight-arm technique for the 50-freestyle, and some are able to sustain it for the 100-freestyle, but the physical demands are so great that most do not use it for the entire 100. The straight-arm freestyle is most definitely *not* used by elite middle-distance to distance swimmers (200 meters and longer).

The following pages highlight the power of the straight-arm technique, but there is a caveat that goes with this appendix: the stress placed on the shoulders is immense. This is not a technique easily or quickly adopted. A swimmer who wishes to use the straight-arm freestyle should have a comprehensive strength-training plan designed and monitored by a coach who is experienced in this technique. Otherwise, risk of shoulder injury is high.

## THE CURVILINEAR PULL PATH

Straight-arm sprinters navigate a curved path back just as elite swimmers do in all strokes. Although Vladimir's stroke rate is a blistering 0.85 seconds per full stroke cycle for the 50-yard free, and 1.0 second for the 100-yard free, he navigates to planes of still water and ensures length in his propulsive path by taking a curved path back, or as Ernie Maglischo would say, by stroking "diagonally" back through the water. Figure B.1 shows the path, from extension to the finish.

In Frame 1 Vladimir extends directly in front of his shoulder. While maintaining a straight-arm position he sweeps significantly wide of shoulder width, and down, as he presses back for the catch in Frames 2 and 3. This straight-arm catch allows Vladimir to connect with lift and drag forces the full length of his arm—from his fingertips to shoulder. To handle such resistance on the limb requires great strength and shoulder stability.

Figure B.2 on page 180 shows the highly demanding catch from a profile view. Notice the strength in Vladimir's upper arm, shoulder, and upper back. You can also see the vortex turbulence—the white commotion—that spans the length of his arm, indicating that he connects with propulsive forces on his upper limb as well as hand/forearm. In this figure Vladimir entrapped air in his stroke, allowing us to see the propulsive energy.

Referring back to Figure B.1, Frames 4 and 5 show that sprint freestylers who use the straight-arm technique bend their arm as they navigate to the diagonal phase of the stroke after the catch. The degree to which they bend is less

**FIGURE B.1.** Vladimir Morozov swims with the straight-arm freestyle technique used by some elite athletes for sprint events.

**FIGURE B.2.** The catch phase of the straight-arm freestyle is the most physically demanding, requiring immense strength in the upper arm, shoulder, and upper back.

than the 90 degrees we see in mid-distance to distance freestylers, and in all other strokes, during this phase; however, they do bend to leverage strength as well as to direct the hand/arm to an adjacent plane of water. Note the position of Vladimir's hand/arm in Frame 3 as compared to Frame 5. He moves from a plane of water wide of his body to a plane under his hip.

Vladimir maintains the bent-arm position as he makes a second, and final, directional change between Frames 5 and 6 to finish the stroke. He pitches his hand toward his hip, as seen in Frames 6–8.

## CORE MOVEMENT AND KICK TIMING

Figure B.1 also shows Vladimir's 6-beat kick timing and core movement on the long axis. Vladimir is rotated to the right in Frame 1 - his right arm having just finished the stroke. As he makes the catch with his left arm in Frames 2 and 3, he begins to rotate to the left. His rotation follows the momentum of his arm pull through to the finish. Straight-arm sprinters must be incredibly strong in their core to leverage the body over the arm throughout the stroke cycle, especially during the straight-arm catch.

The kick helps leverage the body over the arm too. Even at sprint freestyle rates (1.0 second and faster per arm cycle), Vladimir times 6 beats of the kick perfectly with his core movement and the pull cycle. The timing of the 6 beats in straight-arm freestyle is identical to that seen in elite mid-distance and distance freestylers who use the 6-beat kick.

Vladimir kicks down with his right leg as his left arm extends (Frame 1). The second beat of the kick is seen in Frames 2 and 3; Vladimir catches with his left arm and kicks down with his left leg. In Frames 4 and 5 the right leg kicks down as Vladimir navigates the diagonal phase of the stroke (beat 3 of the kick), and then comes the Triple P—the spike in forward velocity as the left leg kicks down while the left hand/arm finishes the stroke (Frames 6–8). The final 2 beats of the kick occur during the overwater recovery phase of the left arm stroke.

Vladimir's kick is more dramatic and powerful than what we see in Peter's kick in the freestyle chapter. Sprinters turn on the after-burners—they are not concerned with saving energy. The 6-beat kick can be delivered at full power for sprints, or it can support propulsion to lesser degrees in longer races. The most important factor with the kick is timing it properly. Always connect the cogs for effective swimming.

## A REAR-ANGLE VIEW OF VLADIMIR'S STROKE

Let's look at Vladimir's stroke from a rear-angle perspective to gain a better understanding of the stroking path and core movement. Figure B.3 shows that Vladimir knows, by proprioception, that his hand/arm faces back on the water during the propulsive phases of the pull. As is evident in each frame, he ensures

**FIGURE B.3.** Vladimir is keenly aware that his hand/arm faces back on the water throughout the pull cycle.

the resultant forces of lift and drag are usable in such a way that he can propel himself forward from the resistance.

Note also his core movement on the long axis. He is rotated to the right in the first frame, but as he makes the catch and navigates the pull with his left arm, his core follows the momentum of the stroke to the left. The core does not operate as an isolated component in the stroke, moving on the axis randomly; rather, it connects and times with the pull, leveraging past the arm, for maximum speed.

The rear-angle photos also reinforce two important features present in all elite swimmers' strokes: Vladimir holds his hand flat and in line with the forearm to maximize the surface area against which lift and drag can act, and he strokes with strong muscle tone (but is not rigid) to respond against the resistance. These details are key to developing the kinesthetic ability that allows an athlete to feel or "hold" the water.

Let's take a closer look at Vladimir's kinesthetic ability. Figure B.4 shows the surface area and tone of Vladimir's hand/arm as he makes a directional change from the catch to the diagonal phase of the stroke. Notice that he does not bend his wrist, nor does he change the shape of his hand, while navigating the

**FIGURE B.4.** Vladimir maintains his connection with propulsive forces as he makes a directional change.

stroking path. The white turbulence attached to the limb in both frames is evidence that Vladimir maintains his connection with propulsive forces as he presses back and moves to a plane of still water. Swimmers must seek this resistance, hold strong, and translate it into moving the body forward.

## PURE PROPULSIVE POWER

We've seen the mechanics and stroking features of the straight-arm freestyle. Let's end by enjoying a view of Vladimir's propulsive power with this technique—his 17.86 power. When the photographer captured these shots, he said the propulsive energy hit him in the head as Vladimir swam by.

**FIGURE B.5.** Vladimir's pure propulsive power!

# STROKE DATA

## Vladimir Morozov, 2013 NCAA Division I Championships

**200-yard freestyle relay (3rd leg), 25-yard pool**
**Relay split: 17.86 (fastest split in history)**

| YARDS | # OF STROKES* | RATE (S/STROKE CYCLE) | SPLIT |
|---|---|---|---|
| 1st 25 | 6.5 | 0.85 | ~8.25 |
| 2nd 25 | 9 | 0.85–0.90 | 17.86 (~9.61) |

*Stroke count listed as full stroke cycles*

**START AND TURN DATA:**

Time and distance underwater off start (relay pickup): 2.3 s, 10–11 yards

Time and distance underwater off turns: 2.1 s, 7 yards

Hand-to-feet time on turn: 0.9 s

## Vladimir Morozov, 2013 NCAA Division I Championships

**100-yard freestyle, 25-yard pool**
**Time: 40.76 (1st place and NCAA record)**

| YARDS | # OF STROKES* | RATE (S/STROKE CYCLE) | SPLIT |
|---|---|---|---|
| 1st 25 | 6 | 1.0 | Not available |
| 2nd 25 | 7 | 1.0 | 19.14 |
| 3rd 25 | 8 | 1.0 | Not available |
| 4th 25 | 8.5 | 1.0 | 40.76 (21.62) |

*Stroke count listed as full stroke cycles*

**START AND TURN DATA:**

Time and distance underwater off start: 2.9 s, 11 yards

Time and distance underwater off turns: 2.3–2.4 s, 8 yards

Hand-to-feet time on turn: 0.75–0.90 s

# REFERENCES

"Doc Counsilman, 83, Coach and Innovator in Swimming" (obituary), *New York Times*, January 5, 2004.

*FINA Handbook Rules and Laws Governing Swimming, Diving, and Water Polo, 1937–1940.* London: Hanbury, Tomsett & Co., 1937.

Maglischo, Ernest. *Swimming Fastest*. Champaign, IL: Human Kinetics, 2003.

Reese, Eddie. "Backstroke and Butterfly Sprint Training." In *The Swim Coaching Bible*. Vol. I. Dick Hannula and Nort Thornton, eds. Champaign, IL: Human Kinetics, 2001.

# INDEX

Page references followed by *f* denote figures. Page references followed by *t* denote tables.

# CONTRIBUTORS

## SWIMMERS

**ELIZABETH BEISEL** won a silver medal in the 400-meter IM and bronze in the 200-meter backstroke at the 2012 Olympics. She is an NCAA Division I champion in the 200 backstroke (2012) and a world champion in the 400 IM (2011).

**BEST TIMES**
*200-yard backstroke: 1:49.82*
*400-yard IM: 3:58.84*
*400-meter IM (LCM): 4:31.27*

**NICOLAS FINK** is a 2013 world championships finalist in the 100 breaststroke, and he placed second in the 100-yard breaststroke at the 2014 Division I NCAA championships.

**BEST TIMES**
*100-yard breaststroke: 51.48*
*200-yard breaststroke: 1:51.92*
*100-meter breaststroke (LCM): 1:00.10*

**ROWDY GAINES** set 10 world records between 1978–84 and won three gold medals at the 1984 Olympics. He is currently NBC's swimming commentator for the Olympics, alongside Dan Hicks, and is a masters swimming world-record holder.

**BEST TIMES**
*50-meter freestyle (LCM): 22.96 (1980)*
*100-meter freestyle (LCM): 49.36 (1981)*
*200-meter freestyle (LCM): 1:48.93 (1982)*

**ANDREW GEMMELL** won silver at the 2009 world championships in the 10K open-water event, earning the title of 2009 U.S. Open Water Swimmer of the Year. He also won the 1500-meter freestyle in the pool at the 2012 U.S. Olympic Swimming Trials, earning a spot on the 2012 Olympic team.

**BEST TIMES**
*500-yard freestyle: 4:17.75*
*1650-yard freestyle: 14:41.86*
*1500-meter freestyle (LCM): 14:52.19*

**ARIANA KUKORS** is the world-record holder in the 200-meter IM (long-course meters). She is a U.S. Olympian and world champion and was named American Swimmer of the Year in 2009 by Swimming World Magazine.

**BEST TIMES**
*200-meter IM (LCM): 2:06.15*

**MELANIE MARGALIS** won bronze at the 2013 World University Games in the 200-meter IM and placed second at the 2014 NCAA Division I Championships in the 200-yard IM.

**BEST TIMES**
*200-yard IM: 1:52.64*
*400-yard IM: 4:00.30*

**VLADIMIR MOROZOV** is an NCAA champion, world champion, and 2012 Olympic bronze medalist. He holds the NCAA record in the 100-yard freestyle and turned in the fastest 50-yard freestyle split in history at the 2013 NCAA Division I Championships.

**BEST TIMES**

*100-yard freestyle: 40.76*
*50-meter freestyle (LCM): 21.47*
*100-meter freestyle (LCM): 47.62*

**AARON PEIRSOL** is the world-record holder in the 100-meter and 200-meter backstroke (long-course meters). He has competed for the United States at three Olympics—2000, 2004, and 2008—winning five gold medals and two silver medals.

**BEST TIMES**

*100-meter backstroke (LCM): 51.94*
*200-meter backstroke (LCM): 1:51.92*

**DOUG REYNOLDS** is a Division I NCAA All-American and Southeastern Conference champion known for his powerful underwater dolphin kick off the walls.

**BEST TIMES**

*100-yard butterfly: 45.92*

**LAURA SOGAR** is the 2013 NCAA Division I champion, 2012 U.S. Open champion, and 2012 world championships (short-course meters) silver medalist in the 200 breaststroke.

**BEST TIMES**

*100-yard breaststroke: 58.32*
*200-yard breaststroke: 2:05.04*

**REBECCA SONI** is the only woman in history to win the 200-meter breaststroke at back-to-back Olympics. She won gold en route to world records at the 2008 and 2012 Games. She has held world records in the 100- and 200-meter breaststroke events in both short-course and long-course during her career, and is a six-time NCAA champion.

**BEST TIMES**
*100-meter breaststroke (LCM): 1:04.84 (1:02.70 SCM)*
*200-meter breaststroke (LCM): 2:19.59 (2:14.57 SCM)*

**PETER VANDERKAAY** has competed for the United States in three Olympics—2004, 2008, and 2012—winning four medals. He is a five-time NCAA champion, three-time world champion, and the American-record holder in the 500-yard freestyle.

**BEST TIMES**
*500-yard freestyle: 4:08.54*
*400-meter freestyle (LCM): 3:44.69*

**ASHLEY WHITNEY** is a 1996 Olympic gold medalist in the 4 × 200-meter freestyle relay and a former U.S. national team member for open-water swimming.

**BEST TIMES**
*200-yard freestyle: 1:47.10*
*500-yard freestyle: 4:44.30*

## PHOTOGRAPHER

**DANIEL SMITH** is a professional photographer based in Vermilion, Ohio. He coaches high school swimming and pole vault and is a certified USA Triathlon and U.S. Masters Swimming coach.

# ABOUT THE AUTHOR

At just over 5 foot 2 inches tall, and not having made her first Olympic team until the age of 27, Sheila Taormina seems an unlikely candidate to have competed in four consecutive summer Olympiads in three completely different sports (swimming, 1996; triathlon, 2000 and 2004; and pentathlon, 2008). Her first two attempts to qualify for the Olympics in swimming (1988 and 1992)—during what were considered her "peak" years—came up short. Following those years, she moved forward with her education, finished her master's degree in business in 1994, and then began a professional career in the automotive industry, working a full-time salaried position in Detroit.

With her eyes set on the possibilities of 1996, she trained before and after work with her small, hometown swim team in Livonia, Michigan. There were no corporate endorsements fueling the effort—just a plan, some hard work, and a coach who believed along with her. Sheila learned about technique, efficiency, and the keys to success. Applying those throughout the years, Sheila grew to become Olympic champion in one sport, world champion in a second sport, and the World Cup standings leader in a third sport.

In the end, Sheila Taormina experienced six different disciplines on the Olympic stage—swimming, cycling, running, pistol shooting, fencing, and equestrian show jumping. Her perspective on the Olympics, human potential, and performance is unparalleled.

Today Sheila travels extensively, from San Francisco to Bangkok to Johannesburg and everywhere in between, teaching the swim techniques from her book. She is also a popular corporate keynote speaker, relating the productivity and performance tools she used as an Olympic athlete to those of business executives across the globe.

Visit www.sheilat.com for more information.